MW01138013

THOUGHTS FOR THE WEEKEND

PRACTICING COMMON-SENSE FAITH FOR A
BALANCED LIFE

BILL SUTTON, JR.

VALENTINE BOOKS

Dedicated to my wife, Linda, who has always believed in me.

FOREWORD

When I was first introduced to Bill Sutton's *Thoughts for the Weekend*, I was immediately struck by the profound simplicity of the concept, and since then, I've looked forward to them every Saturday.

Far too often, we make life more complicated than it needs to be. The way in which Bill quickly addresses the basics of deep concepts, making them both easy-to-digest and relevant, is an approach I greatly appreciate as a busy person. I'm easily overwhelmed by daily devotionals, and the idea of taking the weekend to reflect upon my life and my choices based on the month or the season we are presently in makes so much sense to me.

Bill's wise insights, smile-inducing humor, and unique perspective will ensure that his Thoughts stand the test of time.

I encourage others to follow him on Facebook, where they can easily discover additional Thoughts when one may be needed or when one might like to intentionally step into the week ahead or reflect upon the one just completed.

Elizabeth Lyons
March 17, 2019
Phoenix, AZ

INTRODUCTION

"What the world *doesn't* need is another devotional," I thought (or outright said), in response to those who've asked me for years to write a book based on my weekly Facebook posts, titled Thought for the Weekend. "Devotionals are a dime a dozen."

Don't get me wrong, devotionals can be great. In fact, I'm reading one right now. But, some inherent weaknesses come with traditional devotionals. One is that, as I mentioned before, there are so many of them out there, spanning subject matters and faiths. Another is that people tend to get behind in their reading and therefore find themselves reading a lesson for the first day of spring sometime in late summer. The post is simply no longer timely. Personally speaking, I can't feel the Christmas spirit in late January! Another challenge of many faith-based devotionals is that after reading a lesson, applying that lesson to everyday life can be difficult.

In time, my heart changed, and I had a vision of a

book that was not a devotional per se but instead a few monthly lessons to live by taken from my own life experiences as well as those of others. In 2018, while having my quiet time during a walk in the woods, I made the decision to finally go for it!

In order to write a book different from most devotionals, I decided to have no more than eight lessons per month, going with the theory that people would take from the title, *Thoughts for the Weekend*, that the lessons were intended to be read over the weekend. And, if they missed a weekend, they could easily go back and read any of that month's lessons on any day of the week.

For the month of December, there are twelve Thoughts since December is my favorite month, and I have written so many during December.

In reading through past Thoughts, I recognized that I tried to write each one in an easy-to-understand format that could be applied to everyday life. Many, but not all, were based on Biblical principles and teachings but broken down to a common sense "denominator" that was applicable for all. Additionally, the Thoughts contain principles that allowed those of other faiths as well as those with no religious faith to glean some value. At the end of each thought, a Bible passage is referenced for further reflection, should the reader desire that.

People have said that there is wisdom in my writings. I don't know about that. I was never a straight-A student, I have made many mistakes over the course of my life, and I have used zero wisdom many times. But something Will Rogers said made a lot of sense to me and could apply to any so-called wisdom I might have. He said, "Good judgment comes from experience, and a lot of that comes from bad judgement." The same could be said of wisdom. Many times, we gain wisdom from "the school of hard knocks." I'm certainly no more of an authority on life than many of you, who could also write a book based on your own life experiences.

The seeds were planted for this book a few years before I wrote my first Thought during a thirty-minute drive that changed my life. At the time, I was in what could be called a confused state. I am a believer in both secular- and religion-based positive thinking books and seminars, and I'd recently attended a two-day event with a very famous secular-focused power of the mind teacher. What I picked up on was that the teacher was seeing tremendous results from people using the power of faith. By faith, I'm not necessarily referring to religious faith but instead the power of belief. So, I asked God for some answers and asked Him to show me why these people, with no mention of God, were seeing results using faith.

While on that drive, answers flooded my mind. I wish answers always came that quickly, but they seldom do. On that night, however, I believe God spoke to my heart with His answers—not audibly but in a way that reached me.

The first thought that came into my mind was a co-worker of mine, who said every year, "I'm always sick at Christmas time. I'm sure I'll be sick this year too." Then another thought came to me: "She's using faith in the wrong way!" She believed, and she received. However, something like sickness—that I knew was not from God —came upon her because of her faith.

Next, I recalled the story from the Bible of the Tower of Babel. The people were trying to build a tower all the way up to God. God put a stop to it, explaining that there was nothing they couldn't accomplish because they were acting as one. And what united them? A unified belief. God stopped them because what they were doing was wrong.

Next, I heard in my heart, "Faith, just like gravity or the power of giving and receiving, is a universal principle." God created it within His grand design of mankind. And then I heard, "But using principles without a relationship with me is worthless in the big picture."

The last thing I heard in my heart were these words: "If my people only knew what they had, they would change the world, and quit walking and talking a defeated life."

My perspective changed so much that night! It was years before I got to the point of writing a book, but here it finally is. If there is even one story or message contained herein that helps you live a more victorious and less confusing life, that's the reward I'm hoping for. Enjoy these 100 Thoughts!

JANUARY

∾

Do you want your fears and problems to magnify this year? Or, do you want your good dreams to magnify? Like text put under a magnifying glass, what you focus on and talk about enlarges. Your words will magnify either your faith or your fears.

1

HAPPY OLD YEAR!

SATURDAY

I f you lose all your money, you may be able to get it all back. If you lose a possession, it can likely be replaced. But when you lose time, you'll never get it back.

Here we are on the threshold of another year. Think back to one year ago. Time moves quickly. Where has it gone? Time is like a thief, quietly coming in and stealing another of life's precious years. Looking at old family photographs, watching old movies, and reliving old times in my mind is bittersweet for me. I see my dad as that strong, tough man who had football and track scholarships to major universities. He's gone from this earth now. I see my mom, who was always there making Christmases and our lives so much better by her tireless efforts because of her love for us. She's gone too. I see John Wayne and my other childhood heroes in old movies; they are now gone as well. This thing called time is no respecter of fame or fortune.

My point isn't to get us all depressed going into

another year but instead to show that life can be so short, and time is valuable. Birth is like a sunrise, and life is like a day. And each of us must face that inevitable time of the sunset in our lives.

What changes in or dreams for your life do you want to see in the coming year? Remember, this time next year will be upon you before you know it. Write down a few major things you want to see in your life, and focus on those areas. Read them daily, pray upon them, meditate on them. With your voice, declare that they are coming to pass. Share them with trusted people in your life.

The devil is a patient adversary. He won't be able to come in directly and try to rob you of your upcoming year. We're too smart for that. But he'll try to rob you of today. He knows that the years are broken down into one day at a time. He finds ways to waste away the minutes and hours of your days. Have you ever looked back at a day, a week, a month, or even a year, and realized that you have wasted it? Your future is a series of your todays.

The ultimate answer in terms of how to be victorious is found in James 4:7: "Submit yourselves, then, to God. Resist the devil, and he will flee from you." *Submit* and *resist* are action verbs, which means we have to do something! Once you have put pen to paper, commit through prayer and meditation that which you want, and give it over to God (submit). Then, start thinking about what you are thinking about, start changing what you are saying so that you can change what you are seeing, and start making the most of each day. With determination and faith, you won't let yourself be robbed of time anymore (resist).

Yes, the devil is a patient adversary. But we have a much more patient God on our side, if we submit to Him. Renewing of your mind takes time, and long-term dreams for the upcoming year may not come to pass during the first month or months. But hang in there, don't give up, and don't give in. One year from now, you will look back at this date and read about the goals and dreams you wrote down today, and you will realize that your year was one of the best chapters of your life's story. You will be able to literally declare, "Happy old year!"

It's a somber realization that our lives here will have a sunset. But if you can make a difference in your own way by making the most of each day, you'll find that your sunset will be a breathtakingly beautiful one as you step into your eternal home, hearing the voice of God say, "Well done."

Job 22:28

PROCLAIMING BLESSINGS FOR THE NEW YEAR

SUNDAY

W hat will the coming year bring to your life? Much of the answer is unknown, and some of it is uncontrollable. But what is wonderful is that we do have some control over our own circumstances. What do you want your life to look like one year from now? Get that image in your mind, and start believing for it. Don't let thoughts of hopelessness and fear rule over you. Is it hard? Yes. Does it take discipline of mind? Yes. You may be like me: sometimes, the harder I try to believe in the good things, the more easily thoughts of doubt start taking over. So, here is a little trick that I've learned from those much wiser than I: start speaking what you want. And quit speaking your fears and doubts.

You see, the subconscious mind doesn't know the difference between what is true and what is untrue. When we speak words of defeat, fear, and doubt, we are speaking untruths. But our subconscious goes to work bringing those fears to pass, making them actually happen. Therefore, constantly saying things like, "Nothing good ever happens to me," or "I'm always sick," or "My best days are behind me," well, you get the picture in terms of what you're creating. That is putting faith, which is very real, to work in the wrong way! Sometimes, a belief that is a lie becomes a truth simply through speaking those words of defeat. Here is the good news: you can reverse the process and speak of what you want instead. Put your subconscious to work in the right direction. That lets God's will and purpose for your life take root and become a reality. "With God's help, I am going to defeat this sickness," or "I've had good days in my life, but I have GREAT days ahead of me."

For this year, fight the good fight. Dream again, and dream the good dreams. Get the good images in your mind, and ask God to help you to see the truths about you. Speak what you *want*, even if you are having a hard time believing it will come to pass. Belief and faith will follow your declaration.

Finally, and this may seem harsh, but you *must* quit speaking about all of your past defeats as well as your present fears and sense of hopelessness. What you say creates a belief about your future and brings those things to pass. It can be prophetical. Remember, the Bible says that death and life are in the power of the tongue. It's your choice; use it wisely!

Hebrews 11:1

YOU CAN'T FIND HOPE IN HOPELESS WORDS

SATURDAY

I came across a fellow the other day who said, with regard to the upcoming year, "I hope it's better than last year." At least he had hope! He went on to dash that hope by saying, "But I just don't see it happening." He proceeded to tell me about all of his problems and the reasons why this year would be another bad one. We all know people who "throw up" their negative words all over us, unloading their problems every time they see us. What is unfortunate is that their words tell us exactly where their focus is. And what any one of us focuses on will grow.

It's human nature to want others to understand us, so it's natural to talk about our problems. And, to a point, that's okay. It's important to be able to share what we are going through with a few trusted people. But, doing so should be the exception, not the rule. It is also human nature to want to have hope and want to get through problems—unless problems have become part of one's identity and a way to get attention. But that's a subject for another day.

What do you want for the upcoming year? Hope for those things. Pray for those things. Write them down. Believe that those good things are the direction you are headed toward. But keep in mind: your words will activate your faith or your fears. Yes, things happen that we have no control over; we all know that. But, in some ways, we can actually prophesy the upcoming year through our words. When that guy told me all the reasons why this year would be bad, do you think he was giving himself the best shot to change the outcome? No way.

When you are talking about your problems, always leave room for two words: "but God." Say, "I'm battling some health problems, but God can change it, and I believe He will do that." Or, "I'm lonely, but God can bring the right person into my life, and I believe He is going to do that at the right time."

Remember, it's best not to talk too much about problems. That's simply a good rule of thumb for living a victorious life, not a defeated life. And, you'll have more friends! Nobody wants to hang out with "Sad Sam" or "Debbie Downer."

Everyone has problems. If you have kids, you'll have kid problems. If you are married, you'll have marriage problems. If you are still breathing, you'll have health problems. But don't let those problems be the focus of your thoughts or your main topic of conversation.

Do you want your problems to magnify this year? Or

do you want your good dreams to magnify this year? Like text put under a magnifying glass, what you focus on enlarges.

I Peter 1:3

LESSONS FROM MR. BOJANGLES

SUNDAY

A friend jokingly called me Mr. Bojangles because a tweaked knee had me walking with a cane (long story). But it made me think that Mr. Bojangles was about as down on his luck as a person could get, according to the song that bears his name (written by Jerry Jeff Walker and made famous by the Nitty Gritty Dirt Band as well as by Sammy Davis, Jr.'s dance routine (he used a cane in this routine).

Mr. Bojangles was in jail, where he spent most of his days because of a drinking problem. He still grieved over his dog, twenty years after his death. His shoes and shirt were worn out since he couldn't afford new ones. The singer sings of being in a jail cell himself, down and out. But Mr. Bojangles helped him and taught him about life. And even though Mr. Bojangles was now aged and no longer dancing at county fairs and other shows, he still laughed and danced, trying to make those around him feel a little better about their situation.

I've known a few "Mr. Bojangles" in my life. In spite of their circumstances, they are always making deposits into others' lives instead of withdrawals. They may not have much, but they give what they have, even if it's only a good word, a smile, or even a song or dance. Despite heartaches or losses, they realize that others may be down and out too and need a little lifting up. They are the opposite of what you would call fair-weather friends. They'll "dance" for you in their own way, especially when you are struggling.

Have you ever seen a flower that blooms on the side of a cliff, with very little water and hardly any soil? But there it is, blooming in the rocks! The old saying, "Bloom where you are planted" means just that--even if you are planted in the many forms of jail cells or rock cliffs of life. Not all roads in life are smooth ones, and we can't control many of them. But what we can control is our reaction and attitude. Be a flower in the lives of others.

I once heard someone say of a departed fellow, "He made everyone always feel better about themselves, and about life." I would love it if that were one of my legacies one day.

The most powerful testimonies in life come from those who are blooming in the rocks and those who are laughing and dancing in "jail cells." Anybody can laugh and dance during the good times. But special are the those who, like Mr. Bojangles, help others who are down, even when they themselves are down. You are never in the wrong place or time to serve God by helping others.

Please, Mr. Bojangles, dance!

∼

1 THESSALONIANS 5:16-18

IF YOU ARE A DREAMER, TAKE HEART

SATURDAY

I t's the dreamers who change the world. It's too bad that many dreamers will leave this world someday while their dreams are still just that—dreams. But I believe that, even if that happens, the person is better off to die with their dreams than never to have dreamed or to have let those dreams die along the rough road of life.

Take steps toward your dreams, even if those steps are small. For it's better to have dreamed and failed than never to have dreamed at all. The imagination is sometimes more real than reality. What is created in the mind and brought to fruition was once only in one's imagination. The unseen world is what faith is all about. Did you know that, as we gaze upon the stars at night, many of those stars have already died? We are only seeing their lingering light. Whether you see those stars as real or as dead says much about your imagination. To me, they are as real as real can be.

Words from great authors bring to life the stories

they have written, long after they have passed on. The imagination of Disney continues to bring life, and he has been gone for decades.

If you are a dreamer and people tell you to "get real," please ignore those words. Just put some legs on those dreams, and start taking steps. Remember, you dreamers are in good company. Legendary country music singer and composer Charley Pride said, "I was always a dreamer, in childhood especially. People thought I was a little strange." I'm glad Charley didn't "get real." The result was the reality of his popular his songs, which were only a dream at one time.

Dream big, and let your imagination run wild. There is nothing as real as the mind of a child. The words "I have a dream" were delivered by Martin Luther King, Jr. on August 28, 1963, in Washington D.C. at the memorial site of another great dreamer, Abraham Lincoln.

PROVERBS 29:18

STINKIN' THINKIN'

SUNDAY

Motivational speaker and author, Zig Ziglar, commonly used the phrase "stinkin thinkin" when describing what gets in the way of people seeing their hopes and prayers answered as well as feeling as though their dreams were robbed from them. They may have faith for a season and see great things happening at times, but down deep in their subconscious they truly believe that, when all is said and done, they will be defeated again, broke again, sick again, or as Gilbert O'Sullivan sang in his 1970s hit, "Alone again, naturally."

Many times, great answers to prayer—finally having a breakthrough—are stolen from us by those down-deep thoughts. These thoughts can be planted by well-meaning or not-so-well-meaning friends, causing us to doubt that the good season will last. They will tell you not to get your hopes up, or that your wonderful change in life can be explained away logically or scientifically.

Did you ever wonder why there were so many times

when Jesus would heal or help someone in an earth-shattering way, then tell the person not to tell anyone? This is only my opinion, but I believe that Jesus knew that the person would start receiving doubt about what happened and try to explain away the miracle. Jesus knew the importance of child-like faith, telling them, "According to *your* faith is it done unto you." As the miracle was shared and doubt crept in, this saying could have been changed to, "According to *your* faith (going the wrong way) is it *undone* unto you."

Guard the voices you listen to. Guard the words coming from your own mouth. Pray that you will always be able to discern the voice of truth, listen to the voice of truth, and speak the voice of truth.

MATTHEW 9:28-30

INCREASE / DECREASE

SATURDAY

Modern technological advances never cease to amaze me. I remember how blown away I was twenty or so years ago while at turkey hunting camp. I had the boys while Linda was in Israel. Linda called us on my cell phone, and here we were in the woods, talking to her while she was in Israel! That was an unbelievable reality to me then. Now, I don't think twice about something like that. In a little over a century, we have gone from horseback travel, where covering thirty miles made for a good day, to being able to fly to another part of the world in a day. And here I am, writing a letter to all of you that the mailman does not have to deliver, but instead will be instantaneously received by you when I hit "Post."

People are designed for increase. God made us that way. When God said, "Let there be light," He didn't stop there. He created, and He has never stopped creating. We are made in the image of God.

Here is a somber thought: when you are no longer

increasing, you are dying. Yes, we all know we are going there eventually, but when we don't increase, we speed the process along. I read a study that said that when a person retires and just quits and sits, the average future life expectancy is just four to six years--and that is even if the person retires at age fifty! The body and mind subconsciously say, "I'm done," and death can soon follow. Again, it's in our human DNA to increase. So, even in retirement, people who keep going, keep learning, and keep giving can live to a healthy old age.

Increase isn't just for you; it's for you to bring to others too. Since we are designed for increase, we are attracted to people who provide us with increase. And we don't like to be around people who bring us decrease. In relationships, value is both given and received. But always try to give a little bit more value than you take. I read an obituary about a wonderful, departed man who always gave respect to others, but never demanded respect in return.

Helping others to increase means, among other things, to use the "two ears, one mouth" rule: strive to always listen twice as much as you talk. If you give more value and increase than you take, you will never be lacking in friends, and you will likely increase your life expectancy.

LUKE 6:38

PUTTING GOALS TO PAPER

SUNDAY

J anuary is the month during which people take stock of their lives. Resolutions are made, and goals are set. Our pastor recently said that he was going through an old desk and found a piece of paper that he had written on a few years back. Afterward, he put it in the desk and forgot about it. On the paper were nine trip locations he had written down, describing places that he and his wife wanted to visit. These weren't only easy-to-reach destinations; they also included places like Cuba, Ireland, the Czech Republic, and England—sort of a "bucket list" of desired vacation spots. To his surprise, seven of the places could now be checked off! Been there, done that!

The lesson is that there is power in writing down a goal. To achieve anything, the first step is usually the most difficult. And writing down a goal can be that first physical step of faith. When one is committed and takes a step of faith, providence moves to help you. You can't walk on water if you aren't willing to get out of the boat!

In a 1979 Harvard School of Business study, interviewers asked new graduates from Harvard's MBA program about their goals and found that eighty-four percent had no specific goals at all. Thirteen percent had goals, but those goals were not committed to paper. Three percent had clearly written goals and plans to accomplish them. Ten years later, the interviewers checked up on the graduates. The thirteen percent of the class who had goals were earning, on average, twice as much as were the eighty-four percent who had no goals. More staggering is the fact that the three percent who had clear, written goals were earning, on average, ten times as much as the other ninety-seven percent *combined*!

With this being January, what boat do you need to get out of? Write it down, and take some steps toward your goal. In other words, plan your work, then work your plan. Before you know it, you may just be walking on water.

Matthew 14: 22-33

FEBRUARY

~

If—through faith—you think about abundance, pray for
abundance, and act abundantly, watch what starts to
happen. But also know that just one word will derail
your journey to your promised land, and that word is
guilt. God is not lacking, and He uses people like you and
me to make a difference in the world.

ARE YOU A GOOD LOSER?

SATURDAY

As I watch professional football on television, I notice that there are players who are humble in winning and gracious in losing. There are others who I can't say seem to have the same attributes. They certainly aren't humble when winning, and they pout and make excuses when losing. There are lessons about pride coming before the fall and remaining humble when you're on top, but we'll focus today on those times in life when things aren't going so well.

How do you handle losing? It is a test of character and faith when you fall. Any ol' person can be as happy as can be, yelling "Hallelujah" the loudest when things are trending well. But, how does that same person behave when life is trending downward?

What a testimony it is when the man who has just lost his home in a tornado says that his main concern was over whether everyone is safe, and that they will rebuild. Or, the person who has been through one bad break after another, and is still smiling and faithful through the tears.

Each year, I try to watch *The Ten Commandments* for the umpteenth time. Moses' people handled freedom with joy and celebration. That is, until things started getting tough on their short journey to the promised land. They became ungrateful and fearful, and they whined a lot. So, a journey to their promised land, which should have been only a few days in length, went on for forty years. I have a hard time wrapping my mind around that!

There is a lesson here, not just from the book of Exodus but from life in the here and now. Live with an attitude of gratitude as a consistent lifestyle, because every life has ups and downs. How long are you going to wander when the going gets tough? Forty days or forty years?

"How you think when you lose determines how long it will be until you win," said David J. Schwartz, author of *The Magic of Thinking Big*.

THE BOOK OF EXODUS

FAIL FORWARD

SUNDAY

H as it ever occurred to you that the most successful people are those who have probably failed the most? With President's Day approaching, I'll point out that much of Abe Lincoln's life was filled with what would be considered failures. The list of now-famous people who failed their way to success is nearly endless. Walt Disney was nearly bankrupt when Disneyland was started, and he was "robbing Peter to pay Paul" (not Paul Bunyan or Peter Pan, mind you) to keep his life and business going.

I don't mean to be cliché, but it's true that he who has tried and failed is better than he who has not tried at all. Never let your fear of failure keep you from a dream. The key is, when you fall, at least fall forward. Then get up, and go again. That is simplistic, I know, and the approach may not apply to every situation, but those who have failed their way to success understand that this is a sound and true principle. Never let failure become your identity. Below is a quote from a great movie. Rocky Balboa is giving some tough love to his adult son:

"Let me tell you something you already know. The world ain't all sunshine and rainbows. It's a very mean and nasty place, and I don't care how tough you are, it will beat you to your knees and keep you there permanently if you let it. You, me, or nobody is gonna hit as hard as life. But it ain't about how hard ya hit. It's about how hard you can get hit and keep moving forward. How much you can take and keep moving forward. That's how winning is done! Now if you know what you're worth, then go out and get what you're worth. But ya gotta be willing to take the hits, and not pointing fingers saying you ain't where you wanna be because of him, or her, or anybody! Cowards do that, and that ain't you! You're better than that!"

CONSIDER FROM THE BIBLE JOSEPH, JOB, DAVID, MOSES, Peter, Gideon, and others who failed at times.

TAKE TIME FOR QUIET TIME

SATURDAY

Our modern world is a busy place. Between work, social media, television, budgets, travel, and important tasks such as keeping a family close and intact, there are a million time bandits pulling at you from all directions. Trying to balance it all while somehow getting some rest and needed leisure time can feel impossible at times.

What's one to do? Take time for quiet time. How you spend your quiet time is up to you. I use it to pray quietly, to meditate and see what ideas come into my mind, and to ask God for direction for the upcoming day. One thing I learned a long time ago is that when I give small portion of my time to God, I get more done with the remaining time than I would without having spent that time with Him. I know this because I get hard-headed and forget that lesson a lot, going through my day, too busy to have quiet time. Before I know it, the day is over, and I can't believe how little I accomplished.

Isn't it a strange paradox that there are providential principles that make no sense to the human race but need to be learned? For instance, your money will go farther if you give some of it away; your time will go farther if you give some of it to God; your time will be blessed even more if you give some of it to someone who needs some of your time; you'll have more friends if you give more time *being* a friend to someone who needs one.

When the weather allows it, I take walks by myself in the woods. That's my God time, my quiet time, my prayer and meditation time. When I give that time, God takes the rest of my time in the day and manages it, facilitates it, helps me to get my thoughts unscrambled, removes obstacles, and gives me ideas and insights that I never would have thought of while rushing through my day.

Here's the cool thing about all of this: it doesn't take that long to do! If I spend thirty minutes in quiet time and maybe another few minutes giving my time to someone in need, the busy, complex world slows down, stress is relieved, and there is an inner satisfaction in knowing I've done right. At the end of the day, I'm amazed at how much I accomplished from my to-do list.

Let God help you plan your day because He'll give you the time and energy to work your plan. Take time for quiet time. You don't have time not to.

≈

Matthew 6:33

DISCOVER YOUR GIFT; SHARE YOUR GIFT

SUNDAY

I recently spoke at the funeral of my brother-in-law, Johnny Kiker. I'm reminded of the gifts that he had to give to the world. He could make people laugh! He was one of the funniest people I've ever known. Many people think that the "gift" they have been given has to be something Biblical such as the gift of healing, prophesying, teaching, and so on. But there are other gifts. Johnny's sense of humor brightened many people's days, and I believe it was a gift from God.

Each of us has one or more gifts. Some people are encouragers, others have the gift of hospitality. Even gifts such as the ability to fix things like cars and lamps are important. Cooking and providing food for people is a gift. Gifts are numerous, and can be used to help others.

If you don't know what your gift is, look back on your life and remember times when you helped others in some way, were good at it, and loved what you did. That's a clue. If you still don't know, ask God to show you. But, knowing what your gift is still doesn't mean much in the big picture of life if you aren't actively doing something with it.

Here are questions to ask yourself:

1) What am I doing with my gift? A gift isn't fulfilling until it's given away. Johnny gave away humor, and he reaped the laughs and the joy of others, and helped people in a tough world to have a brighter day.

2) Am I trying to be everything to everybody? You have to remember that nobody is good at everything, and nobody has every gift. Don't let that bother you. Some people try to use humor but are just not funny! So be yourself, use your gift or gifts, and let your life focus on those. If you try to be everything to everybody, your life will be hectic, unfulfilling, and filled with confusion.

Know your gift, don't hide your gift, and let your light shine. Never see yourself or your gift as unimportant. Others need you! It is more blessed to give than to receive.

∼

Romans 12: 6-8

13

WITH ALL DUE RESPECT

SATURDAY

I think that God gives us built in "checks and balances" when it comes to things we say, if we are willing to listen. Words can be uplifting and powerful, and they can also be degrading and destructive. I've learned that there are three often-uttered prefaces to statements, and if we listen to our heart, we will think twice before saying them.

First, there's "No offense, but…" We likely follow that up with something offensive. Second, there's "With all due respect…" It's likely that someone is about to be disrespected. And third, "Maybe I shouldn't say this, but…" Just don't say it! Sometimes just waiting a few minutes, or better yet, sleeping on it, helps us to have the wisdom to know the right thing (and the wrong thing) to say.

Many times, I've told someone off in an email or a letter I planned to mail. My rule of thumb is not to send it until the next day. When the next day comes, I re-read it, and then make the decision on whether or not to send it. I seldom do. I ask myself if my words are constructive or only in a spirit of revenge and anger. When I don't send the letter or email, I ask God to deal with what I have perceived as a wrong. He is a great defense counsel, if you will just let Him do his job. And, the great thing about having God as your attorney is that the work is always free!

Finally, be careful with boastful or prideful words. Many times, you won't be able to back up what you say. In other words, "Don't allow your mouth to write checks that you can't cash."

~

PROVERBS 18:20-21

14

YOUR LIFE NEEDS STORMS

SUNDAY

Who wouldn't enjoy two-plus weeks of temperature in the sixties with no wind? Keep in mind, we are talking about February, when our highs in the mountains of Northern Arizona are usually twenty degrees cooler, with snow.

This week brought us some changes, and the first of next week will bring even more, with storms bringing much needed moisture. The storms are needed because fire season is coming. Our trees, grasses, and bushes will absorb the moisture, making them stronger and helping them to withstand fire season.

Our lives are much the same. We all love it when we are drifting along during the smooth-sailing times of life. We want them to go on and on. But there are also stormy times. And every now and then, each life has fire seasons, times that will destroy a person if they aren't prepared.

So, how do we prepare? By dwelling in the shelter of your creator during the storms. We need to soak up all

He has to give us, pressing in close and making us strong enough to withstand fire season.

Our pastor's daughter and her family lost their beautiful home to a devastating fire that destroyed nearly everything. They built the home themselves, and it was used to help others. Like any family, they had times of storms. But they soaked up the presence of Jesus and relied on Him during those times. Fire season then hit them, literally. Their focus the week after the fire was on their blessings. They all escaped the fire, and they knew that with God's help, they would rise from the ashes and continue to be a blessing to others.

The fire did not destroy them. God had their backs. He will have yours too. Just push into Him closely every day, but even more so during the storms of life.

MATTHEW 8:26

15

ROCK BOTTOM

SATURDAY

I still remember the first time I was on a Ferris Wheel as a young boy. I hung onto the safety bar with white knuckles as our seat rose higher and higher. I then felt terror as it made its way closer to—and over—the top. As it began going faster, I hung on even harder. But, after a few revolutions, it was a piece of cake, and I even let go of the safety bar and proudly showed how brave and tough I was! Always a fun ride, but--you guessed it--there's a life lesson here!

My problem is that my life gets to be too much like a Ferris Wheel. Scary new things come about, and I know I can't get off the ride so I hang onto my safety bar of choice: my creator. That's good! After a while, the ride of life becomes smooth again. I get used to the newness of the situation, and I let go a bit.

During the easier times in life, I notice that I start spending a little less time with Him each day, and my vital quiet time is taken up by TV time, the internet, or the business of the day. I become a bit negligent in my practice of consistently reading the Bible and other good books, and before I know it, I've fallen away. Things start falling apart, and I find myself falling toward rock bottom. By God's grace, I recognize where my "rock bottom" is before I outright hit it.

The nice thing about "rock bottom" is that it can bring you back to The Rock. When I hit it, I stand firmly on that rock and look up for my answer. And my answer is always the same. It comes from Matthew 6:33: "Seek ye first the kingdom of God and His righteousness, and all these things shall be added unto you." Take note of the words: "all these things."

I desire and pray to always hang onto my safety bar, during both the good and bad times. But, God won't take our hands and *make* us hang on. He will show us how and give us direction. He will lead us, but He will never drag us. That pesky "free will" thing gets in the way! I'm not there yet myself; I'm still working on it, but I'm doing better. I thank God for that.

Here is my question for you: how far down is your "rock bottom?" The answer is a choice you have to make. Recognize where it is early on. There are people who don't do that, and they end up with broken dreams, jail or prison times, destroyed families, financial messes, and even suicide. The list of places where you can end up is long and scary, just like a carnival ride.

But, here is the good news: when the ride ends, you'll be standing on solid ground, no matter how far down your "rock bottom" is. If that solid ground is The Rock, look up for your answers. And when you do, you'll see others on their own Ferris Wheels of life and be able to help them by showing them the safety bar and teaching them never to let go. You can teach others about "rock bottom" when you've been there yourself.

GENESIS 50:20

16

THINK ABUNDANCE; NO GUILT!

SUNDAY

One of the stories in the Bible that talks about turning lack into abundance is in the book of Matthew, when Jesus turned seven loaves of bread and a few small fish into enough food to feed an estimated 10,000 people. One interesting aspect of the story is that, to make something supernatural happen, Jesus simply blessed the food and broke it into pieces. He then gave the food to the disciples to distribute to the people. He didn't just say, "Bippity boppity boo" to turn the small amount of food into a caravan of sustenance. The disciples took the small amount that Jesus broke and started passing it out. They took what they had, and by faith, acted accordingly. For the supernatural to happen, they did the "natural" and let God do the "super."

Many cultures, countries, and governments have a poverty mindset. This "lack mentality" even creeps into much of this very prosperous country. What exactly do I mean by a poverty mindset? Here are some examples:

think of a time when you received a raise, were living in abundance or received a special blessing. Did you feel that you didn't deserve it? Or, did you feel that having the blessing was taking away from someone else's ability to have it too? That's like looking at the blessings as a whole pizza and believing that having more than one slice is the same as taking from the rest of the world. If that is your belief, it's like that you have a poverty mindset.

Keep this in mind: we should *want* to have abundance—not so that we can be "fat and happy" but so that we can use our abundance to help others. We take what we have, even if it's just a few fish and a little bread, and we help others. Remember that as long as you are generous with what you have been blessed with, there is nothing wrong with you living well and in abundance. No guilt necessary! The disciples picked up all the food after each of the 10,000 people had been fed, and there were seven large baskets of leftover food. I think it was "pig out" time!

How many charitable hospitals are built when everyone is broke? How many shelters are built? How many missionaries are sent out when there isn't any money to send them? When you are blessed, it gives you the opportunity to be a blessing unto others.

Do you want to have more than enough? There is a book called *The Secret* based on principles that are really no secret at all. They've been part of societal philosophy for centuries and even present in numerous teachings in the Bible. I'm talking about the Law of Attraction. When you think lack, talk lack, and act lack, don't be surprised if lack and poverty are attracted *to* you. If, in faith, you think about abundance, pray for abundance, and act abundantly, watch what starts to happen. But, just one word will derail your journey to your promised land, and that word is *guilt*. God is not lacking, and He uses people like you and me to make a difference in this world.

EPHESIANS 3:20

MARCH

~

People may forget what you said, but they'll never forget how you made them feel. Be like the springtime robin that brings life, but never be a vessel of dread, condemnation, or guilt. Consider the way you want others to feel when in your presence?

17

HELL ON EARTH

SATURDAY

Our pastor said in church, "If you are going through Hell, keep going." I've also heard the saying, "The road to Hell (on earth) is paved with good intentions." Both sayings are simple and profound.

Years ago, I did a series of stupid things, all in one day. I went and cut firewood by myself. I didn't tell anyone where I was going, I went with only a quarter tank of gas, and the fall night was going to be a cold one. Cutting the load of firewood went off without a hitch. I was proud! But it was getting late in the day, and I didn't want to take the road home that would take fifteen minutes longer. So I took a shorter road, but that road had a mud hole. My intentions were good. But I was soon hopelessly stuck and a long way from home. Because of my series of decisions, I found myself in the midst of Hell on earth, and daylight was gone. Just as Pastor Lori advised, I had no choice but to keep going. I started walking with my dog, Panda, who thought the whole ordeal was a cool adventure!

Some points regarding the first part of this story. First, I should have turned back once I saw the mud hole. It was too late once I was stuck. At times, we determine that we may be on the wrong "road." When you determine that, turn back. Your intentions may be good, but something inside of you is telling you that the road may be the wrong one. Your goal may be pure, but remember that there are usually other ways to get there if one way feels wrong. Second, if you end up in a "Hell on earth" situation, keep going. Don't stay there. To get where you're going, you have to *keep going*.

Back to my story.

Panda and I started making the twelve-mile walk to town. I knew the road home and had a full battery in the flashlight, which was the only smart thing I did that day. After walking about a mile, Panda kept stopping and looking toward the horizon at something that was catching her eye. I stopped to look and saw lights flashing in the distance. The highway! It felt like I had to walk across the country, but within an hour, I was at the highway and got a ride home.

When you are in a "Hell on earth" ordeal, it's important to keep going, but it's also important to recognize that you need help. God can provide you with the path by giving you enough light, just like a flashlight, to take one step at a time toward your desired destination. And when your "Hell on earth" is a dark place, you'll know where your destination is by looking in the distance toward The Light. Always remember that you may need some help from others to find your way. Or, as was my case, you might need Panda the dog!

In my own life, I can usually tell if I'm getting off track and onto a wrong road. Also, I know that I usually get onto wrong roads because of a prideful attitude. I now recognize the first two actions that kick off this misstep. First, I find myself not being thankful for the good things God is doing for me. Second, I find myself blaming God for all the bad things that are happening to me and in the rest of the world. I take all the credit; I give God all the blame. And a muddy mess ensues.

If you are stuck in a muddy place in life and are going through Hell, keep going. Get help. Be thankful *through* the ordeal, not *for* the ordeal. Always follow The Light. You'll soon find yourself on the other side of it.

ROMANS 1:21

18

HOW DO YOU MAKE PEOPLE FEEL?

SUNDAY

I fondly remember the first day of spring over fifty years ago. I had a very cool calendar that had sketched pictures of various holidays and milestone days. Christmas had a drawing of Santa, and the Fourth of July had one of a firework. The first day of spring had a picture of a robin singing, greeting the new season. Up until then, I hadn't thought too much about the change of seasons. That was the year that changed. I believed in my heart that there would be something special on the upcoming first day of spring. I got up early and went outside. Sure enough, I could hear robins singing their pretty songs! The feeling I had that spring morning is hard for me to describe, but I'll try. In one word, it was JOY. To this day, that memory brings back a feeling of happiness, and that memory will stay with me and bring me back to that day until my final days. I don't know what those robins were singing, but I know the feeling it gave me (and still gives me). I think that morning laid the foundation for my love of singing birds and the reason I feed the messy and expensive little critters now!

This reminds me of something I have heard that makes so much sense.

"People may forget what you say, but they'll never forget how you made them feel."

That saying is so true. Some memories of certain people can bring me a sense of dread, while others bring me a sense of joy or admiration. I can honestly say that I can't remember precisely what most of them said, but I know exactly how they made me feel. Sort of like my memory of the robins singing.

I have memories of being a young man, attending a specific church for a while. To this day, I get a sinking feeling along with those memories. The minister had a way of bringing feelings of guilt and condemnation to every service. Instead of exiting the church feeling hope, I walked out of there feeling down on myself. I don't remember anything the minister said. But I vividly remember how he made me feel. I don't believe that condemnation and guilt are of God. Conviction and change are, because those bring hope.

My high school football coach, Art Sharpe, was a disciplinarian. He had a way of cutting you down and then building you back up. And although he was tough, he took a ragtag bunch of kids and made us into a good team. I recall losing only three or so games during those years. I still joke about a few things he said during those times "rebuilding us" (ouch), but for the most part I can't recall his words. What I recall is the lifelong feeling of being a winner. That was a lesson not limited to football. It was also applicable to life. Thanks, Coach, we miss you.

Think back on your life and the people who are no longer a part of it. Some of them will provide a warm feeling and good memories. Others will trigger a feeling of dread. Notice that you probably remember only a little bit of what was actually spoken, if anything at all.

Here's my challenge to you today: bring life to people, not death. Your words in the present, which will someday be mostly forgotten, are what start the process. Be like the robin in the spring that brings life, but never be a vessel of dread, condemnation, or guilt. Be a winner in your own way, and show others how to do the same in their own way. How will people feel inside in response to memories of you after you are gone?

Proverbs 18:21

19

LUCKY CHARMS

SATURDAY

Whanhen I was around ten years old, a brand-new breakfast cereal came out. Commercials for Lucky Charms started airing, and they featured a cartoon Leprechaun named Lucky. I talked Mom into getting me a box, and lucky me, the leprechaun was right. They *were* "magically delicious!" The only problem was that I had to eat a bunch of the boring cereal to get to the good stuff, the marshmallows. I wished for something that didn't exist: a box of just the marshmallow bits.

A couple of years back, I heard that you could order a whole bag of the Lucky Charms marshmallow bits without the cereal! It took me only minutes to go online and place my order. When they came in the mail, it was my lucky day. Like a little kid, I poured a bowl of them. My childhood wish had come true! But then, something unexpected happened. I quickly got tired of them as I filled up on sugar. And, just like a fulfilled wish from a leprechaun, it wasn't at all what I expected it to be.

As with nearly everything in life, we need balance. I've heard many retired people say, "Retirement is not all it's cracked up to be" as boredom set in and the weekends became just another two days of the week, no longer special. Others in my circle believe that they owe it to their families to constantly work long hours, to be the best providers they can be. Then, they lose their families. I know many people who never go to church because they were forced, as children, to attend church every time the doors were opened, which at some churches happened four or five times a week. When you sleep for more than your body's required hours, sleep enzymes build up in your system and you are actually *more* tired. Thus, those people seem to sleep and nap a lot, yet they are always worn out. By the same mechanism, if you workout the same muscle groups every day, the workouts become counterproductive and your muscles actually weaken.

Every year I hear from so many people, "I don't need money or things, I just want happiness." Or, "All I want is for my kids to be happy." That's noble, but let's consider the words from Darby O'Gill from the Disney movie *Darby O'Gill and the Little People*. Set to make his final wish after catching the illusive leprechaun, everyone assumes he will wish for a pot of gold. Instead, Darby says, "Nine times out of ten, it leads to unhappiness." A lady thinks she has the answer and suggests that he wish for happiness. Darby responds wisely, "Human beings need bitter with the sweet."

Life is full of strange paradoxes like this. To truly enjoy life, it must be balanced. If "all work and no play makes Johnnie a dull boy," as they say, then all play and no work will make Johnnie unhappy and unfulfilled. People love to fish until they have to do it for a living. Then it's just a job. I'd love to try it for a while though!

These days, when I get that extra bag of marshmallow bits, I sprinkle a few more in with my normal bowl of Lucky Charms because I need more sweetness! Having the ordinary cereal mixed in with some extra marshmallow bits makes the ordinary extraordinary. Such is life.

SOLOMON'S WORDS IN ECCLESIASTES

20

THE HOWS WILL STOP YOUR NOWS

SUNDAY

Before sophisticated farm machinery, farmers dug their rows by using an animal such as a mule to pull the plow. The rows came out straight. The farmer would find a distant point, like a tree or fence post, and focus on that point. If he focused on the mule or took his eye off of the goal for too long, the row would start to venture off. As is the case with many life lessons taken from the experiences of farmers, this one is good.

Everyone should have a goal (or goals). Then, take consistent steps toward the goal. But, how many times do we look at the here and now, start looking at the obstacles, take our eyes off of the prize, and end up going in a circle, ending up where we started in the first place? Or maybe we never get started. Many times, the obstacle is in the mind as we focus on the *how*. How can we ever get out of debt? How can God ever use someone like me? If you try to have all of the *hows* answered before you start or focus only on the *hows* along your journey, you will never get there.

Remember this: The HOWS will stop all of your NOWS. Scottish writer William Murray said, "The moment one commits oneself, then providence moves too." During the dark or cloudy times, when we can't seem to see our goal, that is especially the time to ask God to guide your steps.

PROVERBS 16:9

21

THE GOOD, THE BAD, AND THE UGLY

SATURDAY

It's early spring! Our first few days of spring in Williams typically bring us beautiful sunshine, rain, winds, and even some snow in the high country. In other words, typical spring in Northern Arizona is made up of the good, the bad, and the ugly. My sister, Yae, has always said that complaining about the weather is a waste of time; it doesn't change anything. This is true! I still need to remember that lesson during the windy spring days.

Around the mid 1960s, *The Good, the Bad, and the Ugly* was an Italian western movie starring a young actor named Clint Eastwood. It had a theme song by Hugo Montenegro with the same title. Here we are, a half century later, and if anyone whistles the first five notes of that song, people worldwide immediately know the next three notes. Many people can think back to the particular time in their life when they first heard that song. For me, it takes me back to a summer vacation with Mom and Dad. For my son, Jeff, it reminds him of his first helicopter ride. It's a song that stays with you.

Just like spring in Williams, most of our lives are a combination of good, bad, and ugly. When you look back on your life, which do you focus on? Spending too much time focusing on the bad or the ugly is a waste of time and doesn't change anything, just like me griping about the wind.

During every season of your life, the good, the bad, and even the ugly have shaped you into who you are and composed your own life story. And, with God's help, all seasons can be used to make you a better and more well-rounded person. But you can't do that if you keep beating yourself up about the bad and the ugly chapters. That is just like complaining about the wind; it's useless.

Linda and I were having a nice talk with a close friend about the pain of getting through a tough marriage and divorce. The natural, human tendency is to look at those years as a waste of the precious years of a life and to ask God, "What was *that* all about?" But all three of us agreed that, even in the bad and ugly times, we can learn and grow as people, and become better.

There are seasons, and not all seasons are forever; they change. Not all friendships are for a lifetime; many are for only a season. We had a home-based Bible study that welcomed many people each week, but after a couple of years, it faded out. Many things in life are only meant to last a season. It does not mean they were a failure, even when it's something as painful as a failed marriage or the life of a loved one cut short. In the Bible, Paul and Barnabas were close friends in ministry until they split over a difference of opinion. Did that make the time they spent as friends a failure? No way. Their split caused the gospel to spread at a faster rate, because they went in different directions.

Spring is a good time for a fresh start, just as the buds are starting to sprout up on our lilacs. My only problem with the good, the bad, and the ugly is that two out of three are negative. So here's my challenge to you today: focus on the good, and add a word that is more powerful than any of those three. Take the lessons from every season of your life. Take God's hand and ask Him to take the good, the bad, and the ugly and mold you into your *best* self ("best" is the additional word I encourage you to add). And, like a blooming lilac, you will become an example of making the world a more beautiful place, making those past times that seemed worthless and dead into something special.

God gave us the example. Remember, there was no resurrection without death. The good, the bad, and the ugly from the life of Jesus were all there for a reason and a season in order to give all of us the greatest gift: eternal life. *That* is the best! Easter Blessings!

John 11: 25-26

22

THE SIDE YOU FEED WINS

SUNDAY

I read something recently that I took the time to write down. It was, "The easiest way to kill (or get rid of) something is not to feed it." I've read two books on the Civil War recently, and one of the strategies used to almost guarantee a win was cutting off the supply wagons bringing food to the troops. The side that wasn't fed would lose that particular battle.

Your mind is a battlefield where civil wars are constantly being fought. On one side, you have fear, hate, ungratefulness, guilt, unforgivingness, and so on. You have your struggles. On the other side, you have faith, love, gratefulness, forgiveness, and so on. You have the answers.

Which side do you want to prevail? Remember, the easiest way to kill something is not to feed it. Or, looking at your solution in the opposite way, realize that the side you feed will win every time.

You might say, "But I can't help it, my mind always goes back to what I fear" or, "You wouldn't be able to forgive if this happened to you" or, "I just can't stop kicking myself for my choices in the past" or, "I'm a worrier; that's just the way I am." Make no mistake. You are deciding which side to feed. And it's not hard to guess which side will win.

There is some thought discipline that is needed, but I've found that the best way to feed your positive warriors is with the spoken word. Saying, "I may not feel it yet, but I choose to forgive." Or maybe invoke a scripture, such as, "God has not given me a spirit of fear, but of power, love, and a sound mind." Or, "I've accepted God's forgiveness, and now it's high time I forgive myself."

Keep those supply wagons full of words of hope, words of forgiveness, words of faith, and words of scripture. On one side of the battle is victory. On the other side is defeat. *You* cast the final vote as to which side wins. With this being the season of spring, don't forget that it is a season of new life. And remember, "Death and life are in the power of the tongue."

Prov. 18:21.

23

THIS IS ME

SATURDAY

We recently saw the hit musical *The Greatest Showman*. Although I'm not a "musical" kind of guy, I enjoyed the movie tremendously, especially the theme song, "This is me," and the movie's overall theme, which chronicled P.T. Barnum's early career. He found a bearded lady, a tall giant, a fat man, a tiny man, and other "misfits." The movie showed that, for the first time in the lives of these misfits, they could finally be themselves and not have to hide from society. While some today might consider it exploitation, in reality these people felt worth and importance for the first time in their lives. And, for the first time, they were happy about who they were and proud of their uniqueness.

There have been times in my own life when I felt that nobody understood me, not completely anyway. I was one-of-a-kind, and unfortunately, there were times when I felt that even God didn't "get me." When I was in high school, all I wanted to do was fit in somewhere. I wanted to blend in with the crowd. That's one of the reasons football became my sport; I could hide behind the helmet and pads. My fear was that I would be called on in class or asked to speak in front of people, or that people would notice my unique features, like my big ears. I think that's why I was such a homebody, loving to stay home and not be "out there" a lot.

It's strange how things change. During my college years, I still had the same fears, but I became a non-conformist, not wanting to fit in and go along with the crowd or be part of the norm. If all the guys wore their hair a certain way or had a certain type of popular shoe, I would go out of my way to make sure my hair and shoes were different from the fad of the day. To this day, that's the way I am. To say I dress somewhat uniquely is probably a bit of an understatement. Just before Christmas this year, I saw a type of shoe that caught my eye in a department store. They were blue suede shoes. Yep, the kind Elvis sang about! I put them on my wish list, and on Christmas morning, oh happy day! But you have to understand, I wouldn't have worn them back in the day when they were popular. These days, however, let's just say "you can do anything, but lay off of my blue suede shoes."

After all these years, there are times when I still feel like nobody totally understands me. I don't even understand myself some of the time! Linda lovingly calls me Peter Pan—you know, the kid who never wanted to grow up. She nailed it!

My questions for you: Have you ever felt like nobody totally understands you? Have you ever felt lonely in your uniqueness, even with loving friends and family around? And, here is the big question: Have you ever felt that not even God completely understands you? You know, the one who created you? If so, welcome to this strange, strange world we live in, Master Jack (a 1960s song by Four Jacks and a Jill).

Here is the good news: we are at the time of the greatest news in history, the annual celebration of Easter. According to Psalms, God sees you as fearfully and wonderfully made. You are made in the image of your creator. Your uniqueness isn't anything to hide. God has made you that way, and it is a badge of honor. Once I accepted the fact that God "gets me" and that I can use my quirks to make myself and those around me a little bit better, it changed my life. It can change yours too. It lets God prune off a few branches that aren't good, graft on a few branches that reflect what you need, and mold your uniqueness into one like no other.

As Jesus died on the cross and then rose on Easter, He did it for the bearded lady, the tall giant, the little man, the fat man, and all of the misfits of society, including you and me. You are not just wonderfully made, you are a masterpiece!

Ephesians 2:10

24

IT'S EASTER TIME

SUNDAY

W hen I was younger, I had some self-defeating ways of thinking. It was many years before I was able to turn it around, but at times I still battle those unhelpful thought patterns. I've said it before: wrong thought patterns are working our power of faith in the opposite direction that God desires for us.

Case in point: it was my senior year of high school, and we had played the first three football games of the season. I couldn't believe how great things were going. We were dominating all of the other teams, I was scoring a number of touchdowns, and life was great. Then that thought, maybe you understand—*the thought* —came into my mind and took up residence. The thought said, "Things are going so well. But it can't last. You are about to have the rug pulled out from under you. Just wait."

You can probably guess what happened next.

During the next game, I got hurt, and I missed the next six games while recovering. I was devastated.

It's easy to see my thinking back then and how "in reverse" it was. Things were going well, and through the wrong beliefs, I resurrected the bad instead of the good. I was taking something meant to work for good and turning it around for bad. I didn't realize that what I was doing was wrong because, down deep inside, that was the way I believed. "Things are going so well. I'm afraid of what may be coming." Have you ever been there?

Resurrection gives each of us the opportunity to start again, to resurrect the good, not the bad. That's the practice that is scriptural, as opposed to my old way of "stinkin thinkin." And it's never too late! Colonel Sanders' life was full of tragedies. He was finally somewhat successful with a restaurant. But it sort of fizzled out, and at age sixty-five he retired. He felt like a failure and decided to commit suicide. While writing his will, he thought about all of the good that he had in him, and how good of a cook he was, especially when it came to his fried chicken recipe. He borrowed eighty seven dollars, fried up some chicken, and sold it door-to-door. When he put action behind his faith and didn't give up, his life resurrected. At age eighty-eight, Colonel Sanders, the founder of Kentucky Fried Chicken, became a billionaire.

The same power that resurrected Jesus from the grave can resurrect your dreams, your relationships, and anything else that you may think is dead. There is a right way and a wrong way to think. There is a right way and a wrong way to put your faith to work. Choose the way that is scripturally based; that is the right way.

ROMANS 12

APRIL

Those who you spend time with might hang you out to dry in life's valleys. Or, they might help you to the top of the mountain, from which you can see the truth and the big picture. From your perspective at the top of the mountain, there is a solution to every problem, whereas the multitudes still in the valley will find a problem for every solution.

25

TALK THE TALK; WALK THE WALK

SATURDAY

Y ou can tell a lot about a person's depth and character through four traits: the way they treat children, the way they treat their animals, the way they handle the hard times of life, and the way they react to another person's success. Today, we'll focus on the last two; in some ways, they go hand in hand.

Anyone can have a great attitude when everything is going smoothly. But what is that same person's attitude when things aren't going so well? It is like the person who praises God the loudest during the good times but whines the loudest during the tough times. You know them. I know them. It doesn't matter the talk you talk on Sundays if you don't walk the walk the other six days of the week. And, the talk you talk during the great times won't matter if you don't walk the walk during the hard times.

Have you ever known a person who, during a trial in their life, was an inspiration to you? A person who somehow lifted you higher during a time when it was they who needed to be lifted? That's a person with great character.

The next example is one that hits home with many people, including myself at various times in my life. This one has brought conviction to me a number of times, and hopefully it will bring conviction to you, if needed. How do you react to another person's success, especially when you are going through a hard season of life?

When a good thing has happened to someone else, have you ever said or thought, "That must be nice." Have you ever felt bitter feelings of jealousy rise up inside of you when seeing the beautiful car someone else just bought (when your clunker barely gets by)? I've heard people say, "I'm glad they have received a blessing, because God certainly doesn't seem to care about me." The examples are many and unique to each person. So here is the question, returning to the third of the four traits mentioned earlier: how do you handle the hard times of life?

Let me challenge you with these words: When you can't celebrate someone else's victory during your hard times, God can't trust you with your own victories. Ouch!

The great thing about conviction is that it is meant to bring about change. Condemnation is very bad, and it is from the pit. But, conviction is good and can help all of us to improve. Ask God to help you walk the walk.

~

I THESSALONIANS 5:18

26

YOU CAN'T UNDERSTAND WHAT YOU CAN'T UNDERSTAND

SUNDAY

hen I was a boy and was taught about the speed of light, I would go home and try to analyze how it could be possible. My teacher said that light traveled approximately 186,000 miles every second. In other words, it could go around the earth seven and a half times in that same second! She also taught us about the speed of sound, and I went home and watched from a distance dynamite blasting on the outskirts of town. I would see the dirt go up in the blast, then hear the bang. I understood speed of sound. But understanding the speed of light drove me crazy. I told my teacher that I was getting a headache trying to figure out how it could be possible. She didn't help. She only challenged me by asking how far light could travel in a minute, an hour, a week, and then the ultimate frustration, a year. She laughed as I pulled my hair in despair!

I recently heard that the most distant star we have ever found, Icaras, was discovered ninety-three billion light years from earth. My teacher would have loved to see me slowly going insane while pondering that concept!

I've always been analytical, even as a boy. So much so that it sometimes left me in tears. My grandma, Mimi, would tell me that God had no beginning and no end. As an analyzer, I would try to figure that out. I would ask her how it could be possible. She said that God is like the ring on a finger; it has no beginning and no end. Nice analogy, but it didn't help me much.

I was once part of a group of family members who were sitting around talking about philosophical topics. Discussion points such as the endless universe, possible aliens, and things that have happened to people that have absolutely no explanation came up. Mental frustration started to ensue, just like when I was a boy. I explained my position on these types of things. I said, and I'll paraphrase, "I think that when our limited minds try to figure out what we can't possibly figure out, it leads to frustration and can lead to mental illness." The youngest person in our group, Steven Jr., who was high-school age, agreed with me to a point, but then added that it's the people who stretch their minds beyond the norm who come up with inventions and technological breakthroughs. He was so right. Have you ever noticed that there is sometimes a fine line between a genius and a mentally challenged person?

What's my point?

Well, if you have ever experienced the frustration of analyzing subjects like the endless universe, everlasting life in Heaven (won't it get boring?), or even everlasting

death (atheists suggest that death is just that, death…
forever), you know that spending too much time trying
to figure it all out will leave you frustrated. In fact, you
may eventually go somewhat insane.

I've known people who have tried powerful drugs
like acid and explained the way that their mind was
stimulated to the point where they understood math that
they couldn't possibly have understood before, had seen
strange colors, and had insights they couldn't explain.
What is so sad is that many of those people were never
again the same. They became dysfunctional, hopelessly
addicted, depressed, or brain damaged by flashbacks.
One person I knew, who was the valedictorian in high
school, started taking LSD as a soldier in Vietnam, and
decades later, he could only work a few hours a week in
a menial job because of his flashbacks. He was mentally
ill, and he died relatively young.

So, let me bring it all home to you, the reason we
can never find the missing pieces of the puzzle called
life. God is infinite; we are not. When we ask, "Why was
that person taken away from me so young?" or, "Why,
God, did that person leave me for someone else?" or
"Why was I born this way?" or "Why did God allow that
to happen to all those people?" we start down a road
that can lead to broken faith, bitterness, and even
insanity. It's like the endless universe concept—we can't
figure it out.

Since we can't figure it out, why waste time trying?
When analyzing concepts such as the speed of light,
stretch your mind, but never stretch it to the point of
breaking. Using an old football defense philosophy,

"Bend, but don't break." I try to stretch my mind daily, but I have to finally come to a point where I say to myself, "Stop. You can't understand what you can't understand." So I stop. I return to the philosophy of a Sunday School song I learned as a youngster: "Jesus loves me this I know, for the Bible tells me so." When I reach the limits of my understanding, I simply have to trust. For those of you who have searched for answers and found none, try God. He is the only true answer.

MATTHEW 18:17

27

MEMORIES

SATURDAY

I t's the day of Jeff's and Jana's wedding, so good memories flood my mind and heart. I remember that little baby, Jeffrey, and all of his quirks and unique characteristics. Memories of my kids are all so bittersweet to me. I wonder where all of the time has gone. That particular kid, who had such artistic talent that even his teachers had him sign his drawings for them, is now getting married. The singing and acting he did in church plays and the Sultana Theatre performances seem like they happened only yesterday. Now, those memories of his childhood come back to me hauntingly often, simultaneously bringing smiles and tears.

On the subject of memories, heading in a different direction from Jeff and his wedding, I have had to do my best to learn to focus on good memories. The bad memories of things I want to forget are ones I have learned to put on the back burners. Don't get me wrong, bad memories are still there, because we can learn from mistakes, and we can teach others from our mistakes. And, the memories of times or people now gone are there to allow us to have empathy for those who are going through something similar. Both the good and the bad are part of our lives.

Someone once said, "Right now I'm having amnesia and deja vu at the same time. I've forgotten this before." Funny, but true. There are things in life we need to try to have amnesia about. Good athletes will not let a memory of failure pop into their mind at a crucial moment. And guess what? Neither can we, or will have deja vu and go around in the same circle again.

Memories are memories, but we need to decide which memories we are going to prioritize. I call it "building altars in our minds." We can build altars of good memories, or we can build altars of painful memories. We don't owe it to ourselves to beat ourselves up over the past. And we don't owe it to departed loved ones to mourn forever. The Bible says:

"To everything there is a season. A time to weep and a time to laugh."
Ecclesiastes 3:4

So proud of you, Jeff, for the type of man you have become, and for listening with your heart when God directed you toward Jana. So proud of you for everything you are, for your service to our country, for striving to become everything that God intended for you to be. Today, we choose to laugh and have joy with you on your big day. And you know what? There are loved ones passed who I just know are excited too! And, to Jana, I couldn't have asked for a more perfect fit for our family. We are looking forward to building lots of good memories!

"Our memory is a more perfect world than the Universe: it gives back life to those who no longer exist."
——*Guy de Maupassant*

28

IF YOU DON'T PICK YOUR BATTLES, BATTLES WILL PICK YOU

SUNDAY

When I taught school, there was a fifth grader who saw unfairness in almost everything, and he was very vocal about it, always saying, "That's not fair." Coming in one minute early from recess, he would start his tirade. He also acted as the fairness police for everything he saw in everyone else's lives and situations. And, he became a magnet for everyone else ready to tell him of their own unfairness issues, because he bought in and lended an ear and a hand.

In turn, battles of unfairness started picking *him.* His intentions were noble enough, but he was one of the most stressed and unhappy kids I've ever been around.

A general in the military must carefully choose which battles to fight. There may be dozens of possible danger zones and just causes, but if the army tries to fight all battles, it will become ineffective and depleted.

Every now and then, a disgruntled person will try to bring a bit of sedition and discontent to me—sedition against a church, the city, or a local elected official. I listen, and then tell them that they need to bring it up to the appropriate person in leadership. I don't give them what they want, so those battles soon quit coming to me from unhappy people. People will learn quickly who will —and who will not—jump on their bandwagon.

Carefully and prayerfully pick your battles. Find a few that you want to engage in, for which you can make a difference. Learn not to fight against things you cannot change. And, of those things you *can* change, be selective. You can't and shouldn't try to engage in all of them. If you try to help fight them all, you'll be amazed by how many people will start bringing you their battles. It will deplete you, make you ineffective, and wear you down. You'll end up like that fifth grader, stressed and unhappy.

Television preacher Joyce Meyers recently said, "You can't do something about something you can't do anything about." I'll add that you *shouldn't* do something about something you can't do anything about. That can include worthwhile causes! Posts on Facebook make me roll my eyes sometimes, but I seldom engage in discussions I don't agree with. I pick and choose. If you're not careful, Facebook causes will become your full-time job! Just keep scrolling.

As always, Jesus was the example. He said, "Render unto Caesar that which is Caesar's." In other words, He didn't fight every battle against an unjust government. When He healed a woman from her bleeding issue, it was in a crowd of people. That lady wasn't the only one with a health issue that day; I guarantee it. But Jesus also turned over tables and caused a scene in the temple one day. What do these stories tell us? They tell us that even Jesus picked his battles.

For your own health and peace of mind, resign as general manager of everyone in your life. That sometimes includes even family. Say a prayer for them, and let God be God. Pick your battles, and don't be a magnet for everyone else's.

MARK 12:17

29

WISE COUNSEL
SATURDAY

"Walk with the wise and become wise, for the
companion of fools suffers harm."
—*Proverbs 13:20*

The Bible is full of references to the wisdom of
seeking wise counsel in one's life. But when
people take advice from one who is not so wise
or has motives that are not so pure, that's a different
story, and it will have a bad outcome.

During my days working for the forest service, there
was a guy who was not shy about divvying out his
wisdom on how to treat women. As everyone intently
listened to him, since he was older and "wiser," I had to
step back and analyze how sane it was to listen to his
words, given that he was once again single after three
failed marriages. Even at my young age, I decided to
listen instead to another guy—a fellow who had been
married successfully for thirty years who I respected.

Along these same lines of reasoning, how people can

take advice on childrearing from someone who has never raised kids is beyond me. Many people get their financial advice from someone who has always been broke, busted, negative, and disgusted.

Motivational speaker Jim Rohn has said, "You are the average of the five people you spend the most time with." Are you, for the most part, hanging out with negative people? You are probably right there in the middle, being negative too. Are you hanging out with can-do or can't-do people? Are you associating with people who want you to succeed or those who want you to stay in the rut at best and fail at worst. When you rise higher, it makes those in the rut feel lower, so they want you to stay with them. Misery loves company.

The road to nowhere has little resistance, but it will take you nowhere. And there will be "friends"—sometimes even family—who will want you to come along. If you are on the road to nowhere, turn around. The other direction is the road to somewhere, and there are wise people already on it who can show you the way.

Be careful in seeking counsel. Those who you hang out with can hang you out to dry in life's valleys. Or, they can help you to the top of the mountain, where you can see the truth and the big picture. From the perspective at the top of the mountain, there is a solution to every problem, whereas the multitudes in the valley will find a problem for every solution. I've heard it said that the mountaintop is a tough climb and can be a lonely place to be, but it lets you see the big picture of what your life can be and helps you to see your God-given destiny.

Finally, we all have that one friend who will give us wise counsel at any time of day or night, and even has a manual to show us the way. Even though I read self-help books, listen to motivational speakers, and take to heart words from wise friends, my true wise counsel comes from having a friend in God and reading his manual, the Bible. The Bible tells us to seek wisdom, and all else will follow.

PROVERBS 1:7
   James 1:5

30

BUYER'S REMORSE

SUNDAY

About twenty-five years ago, we attended a convincing timeshare presentation in Sedona. It sounded great! For $10,000, we would own this timeshare and be able to use it once a year for life. Then, we could pass it down to our kids, because we would own that one week each year. Just a few thousand dollars plus token annual maintenance fees of $200 or so. We wanted it, and that was that—even though something down deep inside was telling us to wait at least a day before deciding. But, the cool salesperson said that the deal we were getting was *only* for that day. We would lose if we snoozed before buying.

We bought.

So here we are, a quarter century later, and we have used that timeshare for maybe five weeks in total. We find it hard to book where we want to go, when we want to go, and the hassle of messing with it always overrides our desire to go somewhere. Those token maintenance fees? They are now at around $1,000 per year. If we don't pay up, they add huge penalties and then threaten to foreclose, which would screw up our credit. It was all clearly stated in the voluminous pages of fine print written by slick attorneys, that few actually read or understand.

This is where today's Thought is going: always wait, pray, and think big decisions through. Pay attention to that small voice or feeling you have down deep inside. You may want something badly, but inside there are warnings going off and red flags coming up. Some people think that maybe it's just that God really doesn't want them to have this because "He doesn't want me to have something nice." Have you ever wondered whether, perhaps, the warning feeling wasn't God trying to take something away from you but God trying to protect you? He tried His best twenty-five years ago, but free will always overrides. God seldom forces His hand.

That new truck feels so, so right. And the first payment doesn't even have to be made for two or three months, which feels like forever! But then, that first payment comes rolling around, and that sick feeling in your stomach tells you that you may have made a big mistake. You remember the warning feeling you originally had, but you wanted that truck! And the deal you were getting was only good for that one Super Saturday.

Can I get a witness?!

I was listening to the radio earlier this week, and a lady who is now married called in to the DJ and was recalling her heavenly Senior Prom. The DJ thanked her for calling and then asked, "How long have you been married?" She replied, "Been happily married for two years, and married for a total of twenty years. The first two were great." Oh gosh. I'm not sure if she was kidding, and it made me laugh, but how true that statement can be. That's the worst kind of buyer's remorse. A dream date can eventually become a mean date, and then…well…you get the picture.

What's the solution to buyer's remorse? I've heard it said that you keep from making bad decisions based on experience. And, you usually get experience from making bad decisions. I'm no expert on the subject, but I can tell you that I have experience! Which means that I have made some bad decisions. Like that timeshare.

Here's what works for us: we have a rule that if we are to make a big decision, we will pray about it, sleep on it, and then see if there is agreement. If we still hear that small voice of caution inside, we wait even longer and usually will eventually say No. Three times when starting our present business, we had big decisions to make. Our first instinct looked so right. It would have been easy to jump right in and say yes. All three times, the answer was eventually no. And, in hindsight, having said yes to any of them would have been a disaster. God saw the big picture.

Another thing we do is, if we pray about something and think it through, we start paying attention to what doors start opening as well as what doors start closing. An open door lets us walk through and see what comes next. God is in no hurry. But we pay even *more* attention to closed doors. When it seems like doors are closing when we want something, we realize that God is usually doing the closing. And He has good reason. In my "wisdom" I say, "Every door seems to close. Maybe God is trying to tell me something." And God will speak to my heart and say, and I'll paraphrase, "Duh!"

Not one time, I'll repeat, NOT ONE TIME in my life do I recall beating a door down to get my way and having it turn out well.

Wanna buy my timeshare?

PROVERBS 16:9
James 1:5

31

YOU HAVE TO BELIEVE IT TO SEE IT

SATURDAY

Don't say, "I'll believe it when I see it."

Instead, say, "I'll believe it, then I'll see it."

Results start with a mindset and an idea. Believing first is one of the basics requirements of seeing good things happen in your life that stretch your faith.

As I write this, I am in the Rocky Mountains of Colorado on a work trip. The majestic Rockies are a sight to behold, even in a snow storm like they're having today. I'm reminded of the Bible verse, Mark 11:23, which says, "For truly I say to you, that whoever shall say to this mountain, be you removed, and be you cast into the sea; and shall not doubt in his heart, but shall believe that those things which he said shall come to pass; he shall have whatever he said."

You have to believe first, or in the case of "moving mountains," you have to speak first. In fact, if you are having a tough time believing, speaking first will build your faith. You may say, "But I have a hard time believing first." I think we all do at times. But remember this, your words will help your belief. When you are saying, "I'll never get out of debt" and then pray that God will help you get out of debt, there is no way that you are praying with faith. Don't speak negatively while praying positively. That's like saying to the "mountain" in your life, "It's too big. It will never be removed. Now, God, please remove it."

The tense used when you pray is also important. Pray as though you already have it. If you continue on to Mark 11:24, it says, "Therefore I tell you, whatever you ask for in prayer, believe that you have received it, and it will be yours." See what it says? Believe that you HAVE RECEIVED IT! Don't pray by saying, "God someday would you please let this prayer be answered?" Instead, believe that the answer is already on the way as you pray.

Say, "God, I believe that with your help, I am out of debt, and it's starting right now." With faith and patience, watch that mountain of debt start to move in the coming weeks and months.

MATTHEW 21:22

32

DON'T MISS YOUR BOAT

SUNDAY

Many people wait their entire lives for their "ship to finally come in." But, when it does, they either don't know it or they aren't prepared, and they miss the boat. Baseball legend Hank Aaron said, "In playing ball, or in life, a person occasionally gets the opportunity to do something great. When that time comes, only two things matter: being prepared to seize the moment and having the courage to take your best swing."

Great can be defined in many ways: being a great parent, grandparent, role model, teacher, preacher, or person in service to others. You define it. Ships come into your life in many different ways as well. Be prepared, and live with an attitude of gratitude, so that when your ship does come in, you will be ready and won't miss the boat by focusing on the bad.

How do you become ready? By making the most of what you have right now, by being thankful for what you have in hand today, and by working hard to develop your mind, body, soul, and spirit. Be great in the little things. Bloom where you are planted. My definition of success is a simple one: make the very most of what you have. Do that, and God will keep those ships coming in. You will see them for the blessings and responsibilities that they are and make the most of them. Don't miss your boat!

LUKE 14:16-24

MAY

~

Slow down. Take time to look for the good. If you don't slow down, you will only see superficial imperfections such as smudges on windows instead of the beauty on the other side of them. If you simply slow down and look, you will find good, even during the storms of life.

33

WISDOM FROM A MEXICAN CAB DRIVER

SATURDAY

Twenty or so years ago, we flew into Puerto Vallarta, Mexico, for a vacation. A cab ride to our resort was a white-knuckle one, that's for sure. Yikes! Our driver was the boss of the road, though. I finally settled down and realized that he knew what he was doing and wasn't going to get us killed.

I had a nice conversation with him. His English was good. He taught me much in that forty-five-minute wild ride. He educated me on Cinco De Mayo, explaining that it's not like the United States' Independence Day. Also, I noticed campaign signs all along the roads, and asked him about them. He said it was for that year's election for Mexico's El Presidente.

He was a free enterprise type of guy, and he explained that it's hard for a candidate to win an election if "free enterprise" is their focus. He explained that so many citizens get some sort of benefit, and most don't want to vote against the government taking care of them. But, he said, that year the candidate who wanted to move toward less government control actually had a good chance. He explained that a lot more people were sick of the poverty.

He said that it's frustrating for many hard-working Mexican people who just want to work and provide only to see their hard work giving them back low wages while seeing their lazy brother getting money for doing nothing. That's why, he explained, there are so many Mexican people who want to get into the United States. He said that it's the hard-working people who want to leave Mexico, not the freeloaders.

He was quick to add that many Mexican people really do need help of some kind from the government. He just had a problem with how many were dependent, losing their incentive to work. I never looked at Mexican undocumented immigrants the same way after that (even though I believe that controls are needed).

As we were driving along the shore, I noticed how many brown pelicans were flying around. I pointed that out to my family. Our cab driver used that as another teaching opportunity. He said that the pelicans nest either on or near the ground, or even in trees. Regardless, for the babies' own good, the parents make the babies leave the nest after a couple of months. He said that without the parents making them leave, the nearly grown birds would be weak and vulnerable to a predator. Dependence wasn't for a lifetime. He added that it was hard to understand why some people didn't understand these principles when even pelicans comprehended them.

At the resort that evening, while sitting on a chair seaside and watching the pelicans fly by, I pondered his words. I was very happy and proud that all three of our sons who were with us on that trip were working, even if it was just doing paper routes, yard work, and shoveling. They had all brought some of their own earned money to spend in Mexico.

I also thought about my years in college, sometimes working three jobs to help get me through. I remembered the different personalities of students. Some were like me, working to get through college. Others had earned scholarships. And others had mom and dad to thank, not only for funding everything, including their cars, but for giving them more than ample spending money (usually used as drinking money) each month. Like I said, many of these students had their mom and dad to thank, but few of them showed a thankful attitude for anything. And that's putting it mildly. To put it not so mildly, many were entitled, spoiled brats!

So, is there a deeper lesson to all of this? Yep! We are meant to work and stay busy. We are meant to rest and goof off at times too. It's about balance! And, as I've said, those who retire to just sit tend to die early. It's a statistical fact. And those who do little and become too dependent on parents, a spouse, or the government find themselves unhappy, unfulfilled, and unmotivated. They won't leave their parents' home or meal ticket, even at forty years of age. And they will seldom vote for a politician who may take away their ability to depend on

others. Our cab driver was a wise man. Happy Cinco
De Mayo!

PROVERBS 14:23
    1 Timothy 5:8

34

LESSONS FROM A ROOSTER

SUNDAY

Traveling near the area in Colorado where the original *True Grit* was filmed got me a little nostalgic and made me think back to the original feelings I had when I saw the movie in Williams at the old Sultana Theatre.

I remember thinking how misunderstood Rooster Cogburn (John Wayne) was. And he seemed to want it that way. Even Little Mattie, who hired him to track down her father's killer, thought that maybe she had made a mistake in getting mixed up with him and his hard-drinking ways. Throughout the movie, however, she started to see bits and pieces of his big heart, and she eventually saw him to be the bravest man she had ever known—a man with not only true grit but also a true heart.

Bringing the lessons of Rooster Cogburn to today, some of the people I have known in my life who seemed to be very abrasive and tough on the exterior ended up being some of the best people I have known. And some of the biggest jerks I have known were some of the most well-kept, well-dressed, and well-spoken people; some of them even were church going. It took a little time to see the facade and the fact that their well-spoken words were a bunch of bull.

Look past the ragged clothes, hairstyles, and tattoos, and try to see the heart of a person. Like Rooster, they may not want you to know of this truth, but it will eventually come out. Of course, discernment is needed because I have known some really bad folks who looked really bad too! I have also known some physically unattractive people who actually got more attractive once I saw how good of a person they were. Have you ever met someone who was a real looker, but after you got to know them, they no longer looked as good because of the type of person they were?

Finally, a person, no matter how they look or seem, may need a friend. Like in *True Grit*, Mattie eventually saw that Chen Lee and his cat were Rooster's only friends. She went past friendship and asked him to be family, to eventually be buried in the family plot.

Don't judge a book by its cover.

Luke 6:37

35

THROUGH THE LOOKING GLASS

SATURDAY

While sitting in my big chair in the living room, I have a view out the window of our big tree in the front yard. The tree has a bird feeder and a waterer, and it's fun to see the new spring leaves coming out, then the fullness of summer, followed by the beautiful fall leaves, and finally, the winter look of bare branches.

At all times of year, there are birds and sometimes squirrels eating and drinking. Watching this shift is a blessing for me and one of life's simple pleasures. Those are the most important kind, I think. I'm very busy, and that quiet time is more valuable than gold.

Some people would look out of the same window and focus only on its dirt and smudges, missing the beauty of what is on the other side. How about you? Are you looking for smudges you can find? Or, are you focusing on the beauty of God's blessings and His creations? You have to be honest and look inward to understand your outward focus. That will shape your attitude, and your attitude will shape your life.

When you look at other people, what is your focus? Do you look for the good in them, or are you looking for some dirt you can dig up?

To see the beauty in the world around you and in other people is not that hard. You have to look for and sometimes even search for the good. I have things I'm not proud of in my life. I bet you do too. Do you want others to focus on the bad? Or do you want others to look past the smudges and look for the good in you? Turning it around, when you look at yourself, which do you focus on?

To see the good, whether in a person or in God's creation, you have to slow down long enough to look. If I don't sit in my chair and gaze out of the window, I miss it all. I miss the beauty of the seasons, the wildlife, and even the storms, watching the snow falling and sticking to the branches or the lightning flashing in the distance.

Slow down. Take the time to look for the good. If you don't slow down, you will only see superficial imperfections, the smudges on the windows. If you just slow down and look, you will find good, even in the storms of life.

Who is the example? Jesus shows us the way. Once we have accepted His forgiveness, He no longer sees the dirt. By His abundant grace, He sees the beauty in us, and looks past the smudges on our windows. When we look at ourselves and others, we should do nothing less.

As you gaze through the looking glass of life, what are you focusing on? What you focus on will determine your future.

JEREMIAH 29:11
  Proverbs 11:27

36

THIS TOO SHALL PASS

SUNDAY

L ast night at the Darius Rucker concert, he sang the lyric, "It won't be like this for long." It brought tears, bringing me back to a time raising our kids, and how fleeting that time was. It also had me thinking about life this morning, and how we should make the most out of each day of our journey, through both good and bad times. The medieval proverb "This too shall pass" has a way of making a happy person a little sad, and a sad person a little happy, because of the realization that both the best and worst of times will soon pass. In other words, "It won't be like this for long."

When we enter that dark tunnel of bad times, we have a choice. We can keep walking, trusting God, believing that there is a light at the end and that we will come out a better person. Or, we can walk or sit complainingly, questioning God, and come out a bitter person.

When we bask in the bright light of the good times,

we also have a choice. We can live with a grateful heart, never forgetting the blessings of the moment, lifting up others who are down. Or, we can take the moment for granted, pat ourselves on the back for how wonderful we are, and never understand how other people can get stuck in the mire of a dark tunnel. We can either have the song "How great thou art" on our lips, or we can think "How great I am."

As we walk through this short-lived gift called life, remember that there will be dark tunnels, and there will be sunshine. Each day, whether it be sweet or bitter, helps to form a wonderful gift to the world, a gift that God calls YOU.

It's never too late to start doing the right things. And remember:

"It won't be like this for long."

∽

II Cor. 5:7

37

IT'S THE LITTLE THINGS THAT MAKE A DIFFERENCE

SATURDAY

When I was a teenager, my dad gave me some advice for the job market. He said that if a person comes in just a little bit early, stays just a little bit late, works just a little bit harder than most, and is willing to do the little jobs that nobody else wants to do, that person will always have a good job.

While I didn't live that advice as well as I should have, he was spot on. It's the little things in life that matter. Do a little bit more than the average person, and do it consistently, and it makes a huge difference in life.

Do you want something bigger and better in your life? Then do the little things well. The path to big is little, and little separates greatness from mediocrity. I was looking at the finishing times from a recent Summer Olympics, and it was one tenth of one second that separated first place and fourth place in the Women's 100 Meters. That small fraction of time separated the gold medalist and the competitor in fourth place, who didn't receive a medal of any sort.

Dale Carnegie said, "There are two types of people who never achieve much in their lifetime: the person who won't do what he is told, and the person who does *no more* than he is told." Do a little bit more, and do it consistently, and you will be amazed by the long-term results. You may not see it today. You may not see it tomorrow. But you *will* see it.

What are your dreams and goals? Start taking small steps toward them right now, and take those small steps every day. Do you want to "move mountains?" The Bible says that we don't have to have great faith, only faith the size of a mustard seed to do so. It's the little things in life that make a difference.

MATTHEW 17:20

38

COUNT BLESSINGS INSTEAD OF SHEEP

SUNDAY

The song by Irving Berlin, "Count Your Blessings," featured in the 1954 movie *White Christmas* has nothing to do with Christmas and everything to do with having a grateful heart, whether during Christmas, the month of May, or any other time.

Counting blessings simply means remembering and reflecting on the good things in your life. When you receive an answer to a prayer or have something wonderful happen, you are probably joyful and thankful. But human nature, especially given how fast-paced life is, has us quickly moving on to the next chapter or challenge. It's easy to forget the good if we don't proactively do some things to help us remember. When we are in that grateful place, it's important to try to remain camped there for a little longer.

Write those good things down, either in a prayer book or a journal. Or, take a photo or draw a picture of what happened. Speaking of photos, photo albums—

even on Facebook—provide a good way to look back on good times. They can also be bittersweet, as we look at some photos with sadness. But those times of sadness can remind you that you have overcome, or that if you haven't yet, you are in the process of overcoming.

When bad things happen, as they do to us all, it's easy to forget the good times and answers to past prayers. It's especially important to remember those great things when we are going through times that aren't so great. It helps bring perspective.

In the Bible, especially in the Old Testament, altars were built as a reminder of God's answer to prayer for deliverance or a battle won. The stories were also recorded in words we still read today. You see, looking back on the good times isn't just for you but also for future generations. You decide how to build those "altars."

Unfortunately, many people—even people who go to church and pray regularly—build altars to the wrong things. They remember them clearly and talk about them regularly—their bad health, kids who are off track, and all of the things that make them feel like a victim instead of a victor. The "good" sits low in the back seat, while the "bad" sits on the dashboard, always visible to them and others (and always blocking the view). Therefore, they find themselves always going down a wrong road in life's journey. It's impossible to live with an attitude of gratitude when the altars you have built are negative. Count your blessings, not your cursings. Go back and look at those blessings periodically, and make time daily to count them.

As I look back on my life and our kids' lives when they were young, I wish I would have ended the nighttime prayer with time for them to talk about the things they were thankful for that day. Sometimes we did that, but usually it was simply a time of prayer. I also love it when, at Thanksgiving, we go around the table, saying what we are thankful for. The world would change if people would start doing that daily and live with thanksgiving, not just on Thanksgiving Day.

Although I like to look at sheep, I'll be counting blessings, not sheep. From Wikipedia, with regard to the song "Count Your Blessings:" "The sentimental theme reminds listeners to remember how much they are blessed instead of fretting about short-term problems." True when it was written. True during Old Testament Times. True today. True tomorrow.

1 THESSALONIANS 5:18

39

EXPECTATIONS: A BLESSING OR A CURSE

SATURDAY

I overheard a conversation the other day wherein a guy provided his philosophy of life through these words: "I hope for the best and expect the worst." He is a really great guy, but it was sad to hear that. Why? Because in life, you generally get back what you expect. And expectation and hope are two very different mindsets.

As a former coach, I can tell you that when two teams are fairly equal, the advantage always goes to the team that expects to win. The other team may *hope* to win, but they expect that bad events during the game are going to undermine them. So it is with life. People say, "You're lucky if you can just get by and pay your bills." What does that tell you about their expectations? Just get by and pay bills, but only if you are lucky. Others say, "Don't get your hopes up." So, in other words, don't expect for whatever you actually want to happen.

I'd like to propose a somewhat weird twist to all of

this: keep your expectations high, but not so high that they zap your faith. That puts expectation back into the hope category. To illustrate, let's go back to sports. I've heard coaches at all levels say, "We have to play a perfect game to win." And seldom does that team win, because all players at all levels know that there is no such thing as a perfect game. So, the team goes into the game with hope but not expectation. Then, as soon as the first mess-up happens, they know it's all over because the coach said that a perfect game is needed to win. Even a pitcher who pitches the illusive "perfect game" is allowed to have some minor statistical flaws. Or, take a pro baseball player who is successful hitting only one in three times at bat. If he does that year after year, will be inducted into the Hall of Fame someday.

Do this: hope for the best and expect the best, but be flexible enough to know that perfection is rarely achieved. Keep your dreams alive. Realize that with God's help and your faith, great things can and will happen to you. But also realize that if your hopes and dreams get too lofty, you may out-kick the coverage of your faith and expectations and end up disappointed. Never forget: with God, all things are possible.

MATTHEW 19:26

40

HERE'S TO THE INTROVERTS!

SUNDAY

This is dedicated to all of you who are misunderstood introverts. Growing up, I was very introverted, and would have had a tough time leading even silent prayer! I learned to overcome and compensate, but there still is a part of me that recognizes those issues coming back up every now and then.

Much of the world is geared toward extroverts, especially when it comes to kids. Church youth groups, youth organizations, and youth activities are tailor made for those who are a little more extroverted. The misunderstood introverts stay in the background or to the side, while many are wondering, "What's wrong with him?" Parties and social events can be painful. Small talk was hard for me. I enjoyed and excelled in football because I could play in more obscurity than I could in basketball, for instance (those helmets hide a lot!). I remember a few times, not even wanting to win a small raffle because it would have forced me to go up to the front or get on stage. Teachers, please don't call on me unexpectedly. I'm terrified of not knowing an answer or giving the wrong answer and being publicly embarrassed! To this day, I sit toward the back of the room in classes and hope to avoid being called on. Getting in a circle and "sharing" with the group? Yuck. I still have a hard time holding long-term eye contact, and some people use that against introverts, thinking they aren't being truthful. There were times when I could be a lot of fun and would really enter into a conversation, but it had to be with people around whom I was very comfortable.

Drinking alcohol helped at social events during my college days, which helped me to understand why so many introverts develop addictions. To this day, I don't want to be the first on the dance floor, and I can't tell you how much I dislike it when a DJ manipulates people to the dance floor. I would avoid some musicals or comedy shows if there were even a chance that they would bring some of the audience members on stage. Extroverts need to understand how much introverts hate that, and stay home to avoid it!

Many people think that introverts are not emotional. Not true. Many times, we cry in private while extroverts want everyone to know what they are going through. Family members and those close to us need to understand that we actually enjoy our alone time every now and then. We can be very independent, and will many times go against the flow when it comes to what is "in" in the area of fashion, TV shows, and movies.

I'm not a very "up and down" person; I'm fairly even

keeled. I try to think things through, and I am very analytical. Which brings me to this: if you are *not* an introvert, please try to understand us a little bit. Embarrassing us publicly will NOT bring us out of our shell. It will make it worse. We can be very valuable to the world. We have something to say, if we aren't pressured. We can be fun, if we aren't forced. We have so much to give, if left in our element and allowed the comfort needed for creativity. If you are an introvert, take heart, because you are in good company with the likes of Einstein, Rosa Parks, Spielberg, Abraham Lincoln, and Michael Jordan; the list goes on and on.

Finally, many introverts are just like me, and have learned to compensate. Only those close to us know that we have an introverted side. At the Mozart Dinner Concert we attended in Salzburg, Austria, I found myself praying that when they were looking for someone to come onstage from the audience, it wouldn't be me. So goes the life of an introvert! And so go the lives of those who don't understand us.

Romans 8:31

JUNE

There is an old story about an apprentice who asked his master how he obtained such great wisdom. "Wisdom comes from good judgement," answered the master. The apprentice then asked how a person obtains good judgement. The master replied, "By experiencing enough bad judgement."

WRONG WAY DRIVERS

SATURDAY

Early June every year in Williams, Arizona: it ushers in what has traditionally been the tourist season. And, with Williams' one-way roads, that means that wrong-way drivers are here again. It's always been that way. Their speeds are usually low, making irritation and inconvenience the worst that happens. We used to joke and ask, if it's tourist season, why can't you hunt 'em, like during deer season? Ha!

In Phoenix, there is also a problem with one-way drivers. But there, wrong-way drivers are on the freeway, and the table is set for a tragedy, one which has happened over and over involving head-on crashes and fatalities. Keep in mind that there is absolutely nothing wrong with the cars. The problem is with the drivers going the wrong way.

What happens to us if we live our lives driving the wrong way? Let me explain. The past in our lives is just that, the past. But, if your whole focus is on the past, it's like driving the wrong way on a one-way road. It will get you nowhere at best, and at worst it can set the stage for tragedy.

It's fun to get together with childhood friends and reminisce. We talk about the good ol' days, the good ol' music, and good ol' friends. The stories have us laughing to the point of tears! And, well, I love 1960s music. But time marches on for all of us, and we know we have to keep moving forward in the right direction, because as cool as the old days were, the new days ahead are what we should be giving most of our time and energy to. To put it another way, we live our lives moving forward, but it's fun to glance into life's rearview mirror every now and then. The good ol' days bring us warm memories, while memories of the bad ol' days can be productive in helping us to remember and share life's lessons. Both have a purpose.

I know others who live their whole lives reminiscing. You likely know the type. They don't have anything good to say about anything or anyone, and words spew about the doom and gloom of the future. According to them, if only everything were like the good ol' days, all would be well. Visiting happy days of the past is fun for a little nostalgia every now and then, but living there is sort of like being a wrong-way driving tourist in Williams; it can be irritating to others, and it gets them nowhere.

There are others who, yes, reminisce, but their whole focus is on past hurts, either self-inflicted or by someone else. Their lives are filled with guilt, unforgivingness, or both. Their lives are on a crash course. And just like the wrong-way drivers in Phoenix, the end can be tragic.

Guilt trips are a journey to nowhere but heartache. They are based in a place of unforgivingness of self, which is a ticket to self-destruction. As with wrong-way drivers, where nothing is wrong with the car, there is usually nothing wrong with the person—except they are going the wrong way in life. And here is the kicker that should be a lesson for all of us: when you focus on guilt and unforgivingness, just like with the wrong-way drivers in Phoenix, there are usually innocent victims that you take down with you.

What is one to do? Forgiveness of oneself and others starts with a decision. Then, that decision needs to be spoken. And then, God will help you to forgive. You may have to do it over and over, but forgiveness puts you back in the right direction. Forgiveness is an action word, and it's a decision that doesn't necessarily come with a feeling.

Live your life going the right way. Take glances in the rearview mirror to remember the past, both the good and bad. But remember this: the rest of your life can be the best of your life. Who knows, in a few years you may be looking back on this gift of today as the good ol' days. Even if it is tourist season!

MATTHEW 11:25

42

SAVE THE LAST DANCE FOR THE HOMELY ONE

SUNDAY

One of the proudest days in my life was when a junior high teacher asked to talk with me about my two youngest sons. My first reaction was, "Uh-oh, what now?" And if you knew those two at that age, you would have thought the same thing! But she assured me that it was something good. Let me set the stage. They had just attended the first dance of the year. There was a young lady who wasn't blessed with good looks, good personality, or many of the traits that attract others. So, as you can imagine given the age group of kids, nobody wanted much to do with her.

Back to my meeting with the teacher. She said, "Your boys—I just wanted you to know that they took the time away from all of their dancing with others, and both went and asked [aforementioned girl] to dance as she sat by herself. Everyone else ignored her. What they did made me cry. I just wanted you to know that you should be proud of them."

When I was a teacher, I witnessed something similar while being a chaperone at the eighth grade promotional dance. There was a nice young man, who was just as homely as he could be. As he watched his buddies dance, he finally got the nerve to ask a young lady to dance with him. Predictably and unfortunately, she turned him down, and she and her friends giggled as he walked away. He then asked another, then another. Each time, the same result. My heart hurt. He came over to me, and putting on a tough facade, he laughed and said that nobody would dance with him, while shrugging his shoulders and saying he didn't care. His teary eyes told a different story. I then rolled the dice, and I'm so glad I did.

There was one young lady I knew whom I had the highest respect for. She was one of the prettiest girls in her class. I discretely pointed her out to this young man and suggested that he ask her to dance. He said there was no way she would say yes, and I told him that there was nothing to lose; he should go for it. All the while I was praying! He got up his nerve and approached her, and all I saw from across the room was her smiling and nodding. I quietly said out loud, "Thank you, God, for kids like her." It was the last dance of the night, and he was on top of the world instead of down in the pit to end his eighth grade year.

Those are lessons for all of us. If you have been blessed, always be looking around for those who have a need and be a blessing to them. The hand of God works through people like you and me. It's a strange but wonderful paradox that if you have been blessed in a particular area of your life, the way to keep that blessing is to always be looking for ways to give some of it away. Keeping the blessing for only yourself or the "beautiful people" is a guaranteed way to lose it in the long run. Be a blessing; expecting nothing in return.

Always look outward, not inward. Look past your own family and friends and across the room for someone who may need you. In other words, SAVE THE LAST DANCE FOR THE HOMELY ONE. Your Heavenly Father will be proud of you.

LUKE 6:38

43

MY BAD, BUT IT'S ALL GOD'S FAULT

SATURDAY

With this being Father's Day month, I'm sometimes in awe of the parallels between the lessons a dad tries to teach his kids and lessons from the Bible. After all, He is our Heavenly Father, so they shouldn't surprise me. An example came many years ago from one of our two youngest boys. In his elementary class, if you got a good score on your short spelling test, you received a cool sticker on your paper. He wanted one very much, and I told him that the way to get one was to study hard. But he didn't have much interest in spending time with spelling words, so I knew we were close to a life lesson. That lesson came the next week when he didn't receive a sticker. But little did I know, there would be a second life lesson that week.

He told me that he had prayed and prayed every night that he would get a sticker. He was feeling sorry for himself and wanted to know why God didn't care about him. In my own unique way of teaching a seven-year-old, I told him that you can't pray one way, then do another, and expect God to bless you. He totally "got it," and the inevitable sticker came to him the next week, after he prayed *and* studied. When I saw that he was serious, I helped him, and his Heavenly Father helped him too.

I've said many times that you can't pray positively then speak negatively and see good results. But this was an even bigger lesson. You can't pray positively, or even *speak* positively, then DO something negative. It just doesn't work that way. This isn't a lesson for only a child; this is a lesson for all ages and one that so many people, myself included, just don't get sometimes. Below are a few examples either from my life or from another person's life that I've witnessed over and over again.

- "I've been praying for good health, but it doesn't do any good," (as they down another full bag of chips).
- "Our big prayer is to get out of debt, but we don't make any headway" (as they just financed an almost-new car).
- "I almost seem cursed. My truck just got wrecked again," (from the person who seldom obeys any traffic laws).
- "I want my body to be stronger, and I've prayed for God's help," (while sitting in the chair hour after hour complaining about it).
- "I'm always sick, and I've prayed and prayed, but I still get sick," (from the person who stays up late night after night, denying themselves their needed sleep).

The examples are endless, but it's a shame that the one who gets the blame is usually God, because He supposedly hasn't answered a prayer. But just as I watched out for my son and showed him the way to get his special sticker, our Heavenly Father watches out for us and shows us how to live. If my son would have received a "participation sticker" instead of a "good grade sticker," there would have been no lesson learned. God doesn't give out "participation stickers" either.

So, how do we approach our prayers in a practical, positive way? It's simple. We pray, speak (bring faith), and then do. #Pray #Speak #Do #WinningCombo

From Tyler Perry's book, *Higher is Waiting*, "Prayer is the seed. Faith is the watering. Hard work is the sun delivering the nutrients the seed needs to grow. It gives it the force to break through."

∾

CONSIDER, JAMES 2:14

44

DO AS I SAY (THIS IS WHY)

SUNDAY

As I write, I'm sitting here having morning coffee at a beach house in Galveston, Texas. Many houses around us are built up high on stilts. It seemed weird until I found out why: storm surges from hurricanes. One nearly destroyed the city in the early 1900s and in hurricanes since. It helps to know why things are done a certain way and the reasons behind those decisions.

As a young boy, we lived directly across the street from the Williams High School gymnasium. The gym has a huge brick wall on the outside, perfect to throw a ball against to play catch with yourself. I would practice for hours, using a rubber ball because it bounced better.

Since I was in elementary school, I got out earlier than the high school kids, so I would start my practice while high school was still in session. One day, a teacher came out and told me to knock it off. I wasn't a rebellious kid for the most part, but I knew that what I was doing wasn't hurting anyone. So, I simply asked,

"Why?" The answer was, "Because I said so, that's why."

I took my ball home, and I was ticked off and irritated. I waited until I saw that teacher leave in his car, and then I went and started my game of catch once again. Wouldn't you know it, another teacher came out, this time the coach who had his team in the gym. He basically said the same thing as the teacher before, but this teacher gave me a reason. He said that inside the building, you can hear the ball hitting the wall over and over, and it's loud. Oh, I got it! What a difference there was in my attitude once I knew there was a reason I was being told not to do something. From that day on, whenever school or athletics were going on inside, I never threw the ball against that wall. I waited until later in the day, the weekend, or summer months.

That's a good lesson for grown-ups too. During my twenty years as a judge, I was told in trainings many times that a judge needs to be careful if he explains his decisions because it sets up the decision for appeal. We were therefore advised not to provide explanations. I almost always did anyway. Okay, I do have a *little* rebellion in me!

It was my reasoning that litigants, especially those who had lost, deserved to know why. I knew I had to be careful with my words, but I nearly always let people know that I heard their side of the story even though I still had chosen to rule the other way. Sometimes, I would simply explain how the burden of proof works. Other times, I would tell the litigant that what I heard wasn't sufficient to rule in their favor, but I at least understood their side. What I found over and over was that people want to know that they have been heard and given a fair shake, and that a system is in place to give them that forum.

A study I read a few years ago stated that people want to be heard in court and have their side of the story treated with fairness. That's a given. But here's the part that surprised me: in many cases, they wanted to be heard—*truly heard*—more than they wanted to win. Amazing!

Even though I don't know if my philosophy was for everyone, it worked for me. During my twenty years in the local court, I was never overturned on appeal, even though I sometimes deserved it. I believe it was because people believed they received a fair shake, even when they lost.

Saying all of this, I know we also have to learn that we aren't going to always be given the why, nor should we. When a policeman is trying to keep control of a difficult situation and tells you to stay back, he isn't going to take the time to explain his reasons. When I taught school and told the kids to sit down and be quiet, I didn't have to give them an explanation. Parents are constantly giving orders to their kids, and don't always have to tell them why. Kids shouldn't grow up thinking that an explanation is always warranted. As citizens, we should obey laws just because they are laws. But, when possible, it sure does help to know the "why." People hate laws that make no common sense.

I love the way Jesus explained things. He taught that taxes needed to be paid because a portion of the money belonged to Caesar. He explained the faith of a child, and that we should strive to have the same. And he used parables to explain situations and events, like the parable of the good Samaritan, the meaning of love, and the Kingdom of God.

Have a happy summer! Because "...the joy of the Lord is your strength."

NEHEMIAH 8-10

45

TAKE ACTION

SATURDAY

D ad always wanted to go to Alaska. Mom wanted to go to Branson, Missouri. Late in my dad's life, we were watching a show about Alaska, and I told him I would love to go there. His advice? Just do it. Dad never got to see Alaska; Mom never saw Branson. I took Dad's advice a few years back. Alaska was wonderful.

There was a study of older people conducted wherein they were asked what they would do differently. One of the top three answers was "risk more." They weren't referring to risking the family savings in Vegas or going into highly foolish debt. Instead, they were referring to the old adage, "You don't regret what you did, but what you didn't do."

An average idea, acted upon, is so much better than a great idea that just sits there. Why aren't ideas acted on? Many times, we all know that pesky things like money, health, and time get in the way. That's life. But other times, what stops us is simple fear. Remember this saying: "Do the thing you fear, and fear dies."

Some people, like Mom and Dad, just never get around to it. A farmer who waits for the perfect conditions to plant doesn't end up with a crop. Every day, countless people bury good ideas because they are afraid to act on them. Later in life, the ghosts of those ideas come back to haunt them.

But, you may say, I tried and failed. To you I say, in the long run a person who tries and fails is better than he who never tries. And some day, the "ghosts" of not trying will be harder to stomach than those of failing. At least those who have failed are like the football player who lost a tough game but said, "No regrets. We left it all out on the field."

"For all sad words of tongue or pen, the saddest are these, 'It might have been'."
—*John Greenleaf Whittier*

2 Timothy 1:7

46

GET BACK ON YOUR HORSE

SUNDAY

I'll never forget the birthday when I got my first bike: a beautiful red and white Huffy. Next, my dad took me out for a riding lesson. He pushed me off, and I rode all by myself—right before falling off. He got me up, brushed me off, and off I went again. It took a few falls before I got it. Lots of fun followed.

My grandpa, Paul Tissaw, told me the story of when his horse flipped over backwards on him, breaking his back. In pain, Paul had to crawl, dragging himself a few miles back to his ranch north of Williams. A long recovery followed. When he told me the story, I asked him if he was afraid of that same horse, afraid of getting back on him after he recovered. He said he was a little bit scared, but he followed that up with a life lesson: if you get bucked off, the way to get over the fear is to get right back on again. And he did.

When I first threw in my hat to the election for Judge in Williams, I put all I had plus all my money (and more) into winning the election. I lost. Broke, in debt, and discouraged, I vowed never to try that again. Then I remembered the lessons from my dad and grandpa. Four years later, I tried again. This time I won. I'm so grateful I got back on that bike!

Now, succeeding in business for the first time in my life, I think back to the times I failed in business. Many are the stories, too many for this book. One time in my late twenties, I lost everything and much, much more trying to make it all work. But I'm thankful that, years later, after a long recovery, I decided to get back on that horse!

In the Bible, Peter actually walked on water, then started to sink. Not long afterward, when the going got tough, he actually denied even knowing Jesus— three times! So much for being grateful that Jesus kept him from drowning. Talk about a fall! But, with God's help, Peter is now known as one of the heroes of the Bible.

When you fall, at least try to fall forward so you make progress. Always remember that falling is part of life and part of succeeding. You learn that as a toddler when you're learning to walk. Don't forget this principle along life's journey of ups and downs. Get up and saddle up!

MATTHEW 14:29

47

DON'T BE YOUR OWN PUNCHING BAG

SATURDAY

Many people spend much of their lives regretting past mistakes. They believe that it's too late to start over, or that somehow God has it out for them because of their past mistakes. Then, when something good happens, they believe that it's only a matter of time before "it all catches up with them" and the good things come to an end. Or, they see every bad thing that happens to them as something that is deserved. That creates negative faith in the mind, and some people actually start believing that, somehow, they are sort of cursed.

God does not want us to live in that vicious circle. He wants us to move on, repent if necessary, and look to His grace and favor to make our futures bright. People say, "If only I wouldn't have gotten involved in that relationship" or "Buying that new car devastated our credit and finances" or "Drugs have ruined me." We become very good at beating ourselves up. But the fact is, everyone has made mistakes in life. Do you let those things destroy you or promote you? Do you let past mistakes make you bitter or better?

There is an old story of an apprentice who asked his master how he obtained such great wisdom. "Wisdom comes from good judgement," answered the master. The apprentice then asked how a person obtains good judgement. The master replied, "By experiencing enough bad judgement." There are a lot of people who, like myself, have a degree in the school of hard knocks. Do we let those experiences knock some sense into us, or do we let them knock us down for the count? Today is a new day. Today is the best day of all to start over.

Psalm 118:24

48

THE JOY OF A CHILD

SUNDAY

Who are the people most full of joy? Usually children, at least until they have been "taught" differently. Kids' joy is contagious! We want them to have that. God wants adults to have that too! The excitement for life is very clear in the little ones. So many people let themselves lose that because they now "know better."

It was always bittersweet for me when the day came when the kids started school for the first time. I knew that life would start pulling the rug out from under them. That's the way life can be. It's part of growing up. Their dreams have become challenged or knocked down by other kids, their friends, and sadly, even teachers and parents. Why do I write this during the month of Father's Day? Because there is no reason to try to stop the magic of childhood, to try to have them "get real," to lose their joy.

No matter the age of their kids, parents can encourage them to dream big, to get their hopes up, to smile, to laugh, and to have joy even in the midst of the downers of life. Don't be afraid to be a kid again, whether you are young or old. It's a choice. It has been said that joy is the kind of happiness that doesn't depend on what happens. It's living a child-like existence. It's living with child-like faith. It's living under the grace of God.

NEHEMIAH 8:10

JULY

~

We seldom think in words; we think in pictures and images. As we think a little more, those images become movies. When someone says, "Remember that time..." and we think back, a picture or video comes into our mind. In a way, the past becomes real again. How we see the future, whether with faith or fear, works in much the same way.

49

HAPPY DEPENDENCE DAY!

SATURDAY

Sometimes, the way to happiness is to go through parts of life with dependence, not independence. Don't worry, I will explain!

A number of times in my life, I've said or thought, "I don't know what I'm supposed to do next in my life. I feel like the voices of my destiny are calling my name, but I just don't know how to get there, and I'm not even sure where 'there' is. Down deep inside of me, I know there is a higher purpose and a higher calling, but I'm sort of stuck in a rut."

Then, the feelings of frustration set in, and I can best describe them as being on a boat adrift on the sea with no direction or end in sight. Has anyone else been out there, adrift?

I believe there are three main choices we can make, and two of them are usually wrong. I'll talk about the wrong ones first.

First, you can try to forget about those dreams of

destiny and purpose and turn your boat around to head back to the safety of shore. That's what most people will tell you to do. You know, the "get real," "quit dreaming," "get your head out of the clouds" type of people. And, if you listen to them, you'll find yourself gazing toward the horizon, always wondering what might have been.

Second, you can try to force it by your own will and power. You put the big motor on the boat, put the sails up, and go go go, heading to who knows where. A compass has 360 degrees, and the chance that you'll hit your target is, therefore, one in 360. I've tried doing it that way a number of times, and I haven't found my Neverland yet by forcing it. I don't like the odds.

The final option, the one I recommend, is to let God be your compass. Sometimes you have to let your boat sail and take your hands off the helm. Sailors long ago would use the stars at night to help guide them in the right direction. Let God be your North Star. Just focus on Him and let Him guide you.

During times like this, total dependence on God is the right approach. Your relationship with your creator will guide you when you are feeling lost. Instead of giving up or trying to force a premature conclusion, relax and ask God to show you the way. And, don't ever fall for the lie that tells you that you can't enjoy life until you reach your destiny. God will give you peace and happiness, and He will help you enjoy the journey while you're on your sea. If you get too preoccupied with the future and don't allow yourself to enjoy the day-by-day of getting there, you'll completely miss the boat waiting for your ship to come in. Take the burden of not being there *yet*, give it over to God, and tell Him that you are ready to go toward your destiny, in His timing. Let go. Let God. Happy Dependence Day!

PROVERBS 16:9

50

BREAK THE DROUGHT

SUNDAY

Yesterday, the annual monsoons made their first appearance. Finally! The entire southwest has been waiting for much-needed rain to break the drought and alleviate the fire danger. We've all been on pins and needles in recent weeks, knowing how dry our forests are.

In our own lives, I think we all have times when we feel like we are in a drought. It may be a spiritual, financial, or even physical drought. We may need more friends. We may feel as though we are isolated on a deserted island. We need God to "rain" down on our lives and water the areas affected by drought.

How do we break these droughts when they come upon us? One of the best pieces of advice I've ever heard is, when you continue to be thankful and let your words be filled with gratitude, even during times of drought, that gratitude pokes holes in the rainclouds of blessings, letting God rain down on you exactly what you need.

Living with an attitude of gratitude is what causes blessings to rain down, while living with a bad attitude attracts drought into your life. All of us have bad attitudes at times. We complain, worry, gossip, and speak negatively about almost everything. Before we know it, we are in a drought. When we are in a drought, we are in a weakened state, just like the trees that are in need of rain. We are in no position to fight off any of life's fires that come upon us. They can destroy a person, just like fire destroys our forests. That's why there are countless examples of people who had so much potential when they were young and were so great to be around. But, over the years, a constant negative attitude full of complaining, worrying, and gossiping took over, and now they are bitter, negative, and even mean.

But here is the good news—no, the GREAT news! We have a choice, and it's never too late to start over. Ask God to help you change your attitude. Start speaking words of praise, especially during times of drought, and then never forget to be thankful for the rains that come into your life.

The choice is simple: live with gratitude, not an attitude.

PHILIPPIANS 4:6

51

BE A DOER

SATURDAY

I n this world, there are dreamers, planners, and doers. The people who get things done are a bit of each, and the ones who rise above the crowd are all three—but they especially possess the "doer" component. They don't wait for the spirit to move them; they move the spirit.

You may have the greatest dreams and the greatest plans, and may be in the center of God's will, but until you "do," you'll stay where you are. God expects us to step out in faith, not sit back in fear. Does stepping out in faith guarantee success? Of course not. But don't let being afraid stop you. You can't wring your hands and roll up your sleeves at the same time!

Recently, my son Brent launched into a new hobby: easel painting. The advice he received was to just start putting paint to paper. "Let that be your outlet, and open up your creativity," he was told. Productive and great writers know that a way to cure writer's block is to simply start writing. Composers need to start composing. "Just Do It" isn't just for Nike!

Let me qualify all of this by saying that not all seasons are seasons for doing. I've known many great doers who got out of balance, experienced burnout, and watched as they and their families suffered. Some ended up dying young because of stress, alcohol, or drug-related illnesses. Don't forget that some of the best ideas come from seasons of rest and quiet.

Stay in balance. But when you know you have that great idea and a great plan, don't wait for the spirit to move you; move the spirit instead.

"…the moment one definitely commits oneself, then Providence moves too. All sorts of things occur to help one that would never otherwise have occurred." — *William Hutchinson Murray*

JAMES 1:22

52

A TALE OF TWO BOSSES

SUNDAY

During my college days, I worked for the forest service during summer breaks. I worked on engineering survey crews during two summers, and on firefighting crews during the other summers. I had a number of supervisors over the years, many of them good, some of them not so good. One of them was a nightmare. He tried to motivate people by embarrassing or humiliating them, especially if he could do it in front of others. Putting people down was his modus operandi. He loved to make himself look smart by making fun of others in a not-so-good-natured way. And he was especially fond of talking badly about a person when that person wasn't around. He always got a lot of laughs from others who had the same mindset.

During times of hard work, he never dove in and just did the work. He took his role of "supervisor" to the extreme, and words of criticism were always freely flowing, as were words of gossip, embarrassment, humiliation, and division. That was his form of leading.

He loved telling people what *not* to do, with no explanation as to why. Boss was his name, power was his game.

Contrast that with one of my first engineering supervisors. He stressed teamwork with our crew, and his method of leading made us into a sort of family at work. He would never embarrass anyone in front of others, and if someone did something wrong, he would simply show them the right way to do it. When something was done correctly, words of praise always flowed freely. We played great card games on the ground in the shade of a big pine tree during our lunch hour, and the workday was actually a lot of fun. He was the hardest worker on our crew, leading by example.

One thing he did that I loved was, he set a goal for the day. Mind you, it would be a pretty lofty goal, but he told us that if we could reach that goal, we could quit an hour before quitting time, sit under a shady tree, and continue our lunchtime card game during the last hour of work. Our crew became a well-oiled machine, moving quickly down the country roads.

The results of the two crews were strikingly different. The first crew accomplished very little beyond bickering, gossiping, and humiliating. The second crew set survey records! We were commended after a few weeks by the higher ups for surveying more miles in a month than any other crew ever had. Teamwork, praise, unity, respect, and all-around good leadership made the difference as we worked hard to achieve our goals.

I consider it a blessing to have been on crews with those two leadership extremes. It helped me so much as a dad, husband, school teacher, judge, and president of various groups. We can learn from good examples, but we can also learn from bad examples. Wisdom can be gained from both.

The Bible says "Train up a child in the way he should go......" Isn't it interesting that it never says to train up a child in the ways he *shouldn't* go? The Bible says that loving discipline is needed for those things that one should not do. And the Bible also says that we should not provoke our children (we're their first supervisor) so that they will not become discouraged.

Whether it be as a parent, a grandparent, in the workplace, or in clubs or church, each of us has times when we are leaders. What type of leader do you want to be?

~

COLOSSIANS 3:21

53

SERVICE FIRST

SATURDAY

Many years ago, my dad taught me a lesson I've tried to live by ever since. He was a police officer at the time, and he said that if you can treat a person with respect and as a human being, even if you are making an arrest, the process almost always goes better. Police officers who don't forget the human element and remember "service first" are almost always the best officers.

One morning at the courthouse, we had bought some doughnuts as a treat. The sheriff had brought over a couple of inmates from the jail for their court appearances. When I entered the courtroom, the deputy sheriff and the inmates were all eating doughnuts! Kathie made sure that all were made to feel welcome and given respect, even while in handcuffs. Service first!

Recently, I found out that a certain utility company in a bigger city had forgotten the concept of "service first." If you pay your bill automatically from your debit card and it is declined once, you must pay in person (and in cash) from that point. That's putting service last. Since I don't live there, it didn't affect me, but every time I get my debit card replaced or renewed, there are places where I forget about automatic payments that need to be updated, and the service establishments let me know that my card was declined. That's human.

We live in a world that is going more and more toward a "service last" approach. I visit courts all over the state, and unfortunately there are some courts that actually foster a level of disrespect. Many businesses are the same way. And some MVD offices, well, don't get me started! Strict adherences to company policies generally ignores the human element and the human situation an individual may have.

That's why, when I started our business, one thing I stressed (and still stress) is the importance of respect and service. There is a human being behind that case number. Not all people will give respect back, but most do. I think they are pleasantly surprised when words of understanding are on the other end of the phone line. Our company policies are flexible to bend with an individual's situation. People first, not policy first.

Putting service first creates respect and helps people find dignity. A fair shake is all most people are looking for. And, many times, folks are more interested in being heard and actually listened to than winning.

I believe that givers have good things come back their direction as well. Regardless, it's a solid way to live: service first.

I would love to see it make a comeback, so that company policy transforms back to people policy.

Luke 6:38

54

MY MOM'S HOPE

SUNDAY

It was eighteen years ago today that one of the greatest people I have ever known, my mom, passed along to her Heavenly home. Time passes so quickly.

My mom had been sent home from the doctor, and because of complications from kidney failure, had been given between one to ten days to live. The doctor said there was no hope. And, wouldn't you know it, Mom died on the tenth day. She was strong! We all had some great times with her during those last days. I'll always be grateful for that.

As Mom knew her time with us was no longer measured in years, but instead in days, her hope for getting well was no more. But Mom still had hope. She had hope that this place called Heaven was real, and that it was everything she'd heard it was. She had hope that she was close to seeing her departed family, including her daughter, Sue, once again. And, if you knew Mom, you knew that her concern was with us, the ones she would leave behind. She had hope that we would all be okay and would be together once again someday.

Everyone has hope. Even those who have lost all hope still have it deep down inside. And, although hope is good, we need to transition from hope to faith; they are different. The Bible says that faith is the substance of things hoped for (Hebrews 11:1). Mom transitioned from hope to faith during her final days. Let me explain how.

You can hope for all kinds of things, but without faith, hope doesn't mean much, even though it's vital to our sanity. You may say, "I hope our financial situation gets better." But, without faith, those are just words, and they hold little power. Until you start to believe, hope is just that—hope. Writing in a greeting card, "We're hoping for a quick recovery from your sickness" is nice, but when you get right down to it, it doesn't mean much more than saying "We haven't forgotten about you." How about instead writing "We're *believing* for a quick recovery." That puts faith behind your words.

The whole Bible verse says, "Faith is the substance of things hoped for, the evidence of things not seen." You see, faith goes to work in the world of the unseen, bringing about what you are hoping for. What is the unseen world? Well, I haven't seen it because it's unseen! But, for me, it's God, angels, and even the power we have, deep in our subconscious minds. Faith gets hope going in the right direction, toward answers.

So then, how do we acquire something so valuable as faith? Let's go back to Mom's last days. She asked me to read to her from the Bible every night. I found verses about hope and faith, about Heaven, and about Jesus' love. It was the first time in her life that she asked me to read to her from the Bible. She seldom read it to herself; I could rarely even get Mom to go to church with me, but I know she prayed every day. She didn't talk about it much. That just wasn't her style. But she instinctively knew that she needed faith, not just hope. And although she didn't know it, by reading the Bible, she was putting the words in her subconscious that would build faith. Without knowing it, she was putting into action another Bible verse, this one from Romans 10:17: "So then faith cometh by hearing, and hearing by the word of God."

Every day, she heard God's word and her faith grew. It grew to the point of her seeing an angel in her room, an angel that none of us could see. She said he was "big," and I firmly believe that he was sent to help Mom with her transition.

In conclusion, it's important to look at that last Bible verse again. Notice that it says we get faith by *hearing* the word of God. Hearing is present tense. It doesn't say "by having heard." I believe that is why it's important for us to have a daily time of prayer, letting God "talk" to us in quiet time, and doing some Bible reading. It only takes a few minutes, but building your faith daily is the most important exercise you will ever do. As I think Mom would say now, "No hope? No way! Have faith."

∼

MATTHEW 21:22

55

UNFORGIVINGNESS: A POWERFUL POISON

SATURDAY

There are two ways to poison vegetation. One is to kill all vegetation. The other is to kill only weeds, but not harm lawns. Last summer, I thought I used spot weed killer in my back yard, then realized that I had used the total vegetation killer instead. It not only killed the weeds but also the grass for six inches around every weed. My backyard still has bare patches a year later!

So it is with unforgivingness and hate. It will eventually destroy not only you but also those around you who you love. Plus, the target of your unforgivingness either won't know or won't care. Like Tim Allen said on the show *Last Man Standing*, "Unforgivingness is like drinking poison and hoping the other person dies."

One psychologist said, "There would be little need for my services if people would destroy negative thoughts *before* they became mental monsters."

"But you don't understand," you may say. "I have

every right and should hate this person. And forgiveness is out of the question." What do you do? The power of unforgivingness, then forgiveness, was delivered masterfully in the book and movie *The Shack*. It is not a feeling; it's purposely speaking and thinking forgiveness. It doesn't have to be said to the other person, but it must be spoken and thought. And it's usually a process, not an instantaneous event.

Once again, God has given us the template. His only son was murdered with unspeakable cruelty. But He forgave so that all of our sins would be forgiven. Jesus even asked for forgiveness for those who were killing Him, while He was in the midst of agony. We simply have to give and receive forgiveness in return.

The recent rains are starting to allow the bare spots in my lawn to fill in with new grass. So it is when we trade hate and unforgivingness for love and forgiveness. It's a process, but you will get well, and that will help those around you too.

Finally, there are times when you need to forgive the person who is the hardest to forgive: yourself. Jesus took care of that already. Receive it! By letting His grace and mercy rain down on you, and then doing the same for others, it lets those dead places in your life begin to fill in and heal.

∽

MATTHEW 6:15

56

MAKING MOVIES

SUNDAY

Another year has come and gone, and I'm another year older! It seems like it was only five years ago that *The Titanic* and *Men in Black* were released, yet it was twenty years ago! Today is the future that seemed so far away two decades ago.

As I ponder the past, a thought came to mind: we seldom think in words; we think in pictures and images. As we think a little more, those still images become movies. When someone says, "Remember that time…" and we think back, a picture or video comes into our heads. In a way, the past becomes real again. The future can work in the same manner. When words are spoken about your future, either your own words or someone else's, you often start seeing a picture in your mind. In time, those pictures can become movies.

If you "see" yourself as broke, sick, and distraught, that becomes a movie in the mind. And there is a good chance that what you "see" will become real in the future. Scary, huh? But, this is simply an example of using our power of faith in the wrong way.

As a teacher, I had my share of failures. I wish I had changed the way I taught a few of the kids. But, I had some successes too. One boy in particular comes to mind. He was brought to me by another teacher who couldn't handle him. I noticed that this student was a leader, but a leader in the wrong way. He would take a bunch of students down the wrong path. First of all, I showed him love, and I showed him that I really liked him. I may have lied a little, but I faked it well. I then met with him before school one day and told him how much of a leader he was. I also told him that he was making my life tough because he was leading in the wrong way. I started painting a picture in his mind that he was a leader, and he could have a good impact as a good leader.

The transition was gradual, but it was also dramatic. One day, he met with me privately and told me that he had been told all his life that he was a bad boy. He even had a shirt that his mom had bought for him with the words "Bad Boy Club" printed on it. He said people had told him that he would never amount to anything. When I showed him love and that I believed in his ability to be a great leader, his life changed. In a school year's time, he was seeing a different "movie" about his future life. He's a successful man and leader today.

That's why it's imperative to surround yourself, as much as possible, with people who bring you hope instead of defeat. I'm hoping this story challenges you to be a person who brings hope to others. When we speak into others' lives, we either add value or we burden them. The same can be said about the way we speak to ourselves. We get an image in our mind as we speak our words, and then those images will become movies that bring us faith—in either the right or wrong way. In other words, they become previews of coming attractions.

MARK 11:24

AUGUST

~

Life is not a courtroom wherein only the facts matter.
God has a truth about you, and He renders a verdict in
your favor every time, but only if you are open to
receive that verdict. Always remember, the facts are
what *you* see. The truth is what *God* sees. And what he
sees of you is so much better than what you see of
yourself. Let Him show you a true reflection of you, by
faith.

57

THERE ARE NO SHORTCUTS TO GOOD HEALTH

SATURDAY

A few years ago, I was asked to be in a dodgeball tournament. Of course I said yes, but being somewhat out of shape at the time, I decided that I had better do some running and stretching for a few days before the event. In the very first game, I made a quick move and tore my calf muscle. I hobbled around and finished the tournament, but by that night I couldn't even get up the stairs without a lot of pain. It took a month to recover.

There are very few shortcuts in life. Today, let's use weight loss as an example. Why weight loss? Because US national health stats show that nearly three quarters of men and nearly two thirds of women are overweight. And few are that way because of a medical condition.

Have you ever known someone who gets on a fad diet or quick weight loss diet and sees big results in a short time, only to see all of that weight and more come back fairly quickly? Here is the problem: when you lose weight quickly, it messes with your metabolism and your body "talks" to your subconscious when you lose all that weight. It tells the mind that you are in starvation mode and that you need to start adding more fat for survival. Thus a plateau—or even a weight gain—happens, leading to frustration. What's even worse is that when you get off the diet, more fat is usually added. It's no wonder why people give up.

Here is the good news: it can work in the other direction too. But remember, there are few true shortcuts in life. How many calories does the average adult burn in a day? It varies by age, size, and sex, but let's just start with myself. I burn about 2,300 calories a day. So, with no exercise, if I consume 2,300 calories in a day, there is no change to my weight. There are about 3,600 calories in each pound of fat. So, if I consume only 100 extra calories every day, in just thirty-six days, I will have gained about one pound. In a year, I will have gained about ten pounds. Now take that over three, four, or five years, and it's easy to see why Americans have weight problems.

Turning it around, when we cut back on our eating, even just a bit, and do a little exercise each day, good change can happen. But again, there are few shortcuts in life. When a person tries and then only sees a weight loss of two pounds in the first month, they often give up. But, over a year, that would be a twenty-four pound loss!

First, decide what your body's weight should be. I bet you already know that. And by the way, don't look at those medical and insurance weight charts, because people have different body types and many of those charts don't take into account skeletal build, muscle tone, and the weight that works for you. Your ideal weight is *your* ideal weight. It varies by person, but it's a weight at which you are the most healthy and feel your best.

Once you have a goal, set out to lose two or three pounds a month, and stick with it. Your body will then tell your subconscious that things are running pretty smoothly, and everything will adjust nicely over time. As a famous preacher once said, "Inch by inch, anything is a cinch!"

3 John 1:2

58

FACTS VERSUS TRUTH

SUNDAY

There was a year in my life when I knew a lady in her eighties, and she wasn't in the best of health. During that same year, I knew a man who was also in his eighties, also not in the best of health. But, their outlooks on life were totally different. The man saw the facts only, that he was old and not in good health. The woman looked past the facts to the truth. Let me explain.

The man said, "I'm old, sick, and tired. I'm no good for anything anymore." The woman said, "I am going to live, I mean *live*, until I die. Every day God has something for me and someone I can help." The man didn't live long, and he died bitter. The woman lived for quite a few more years, and she *lived* until the last few days of her life. Her health even improved! God had a truth and a plan for both of them. Only one chose to receive it.

Facts are what you see. Truth is what God sees. It may be factual that you are broke and in debt. But if you trust Him, God has a truth about you: you will be financially free. Why? Because He loves you and wants the best for you. Even more importantly, He wants you to have more than enough so that you can be a blessing to others, more of a blessing than you can be today. The truth really does set you free. That freedom may be seen in an older lady living out her days in joy and peace. That freedom may be seen as you, living your future without so much stress. God wants you to "prosper and be in health."

It's too bad that so many people never get to see the truth because they see only the facts, and those facts become their identity. They say, "I'll never get out of debt" or "I'll never amount to anything" or "Nobody would ever love someone like me." By declaring and decreeing those statements, they undo all of the asking, praying, and even begging God to get them out of their circumstances. You can't ask for one thing, then declare another and expect to see changes. That is practicing faith in the wrong way.

Life is not a courtroom where only the facts matter. God has a truth about you, and He renders a verdict in your favor every time, but only if you receive that verdict. Always remember, the facts are what *you* see. The truth is what *God* sees. And what he sees of you is so much better than what you see. Let Him show you a true reflection of you, by faith.

∾

JOHN 8:32

59

A CHILDLIKE HEART

SATURDAY

This week I saw the new Disney movie, *Christopher Robin*. It brought back a memory of my niece, Kellie, from when she was a little girl. Winnie the Pooh was her stuffed animal, and she couldn't live without it. Everywhere she went, Pooh had to be with her. When the family made their first trip to Disneyland, upon seeing Winnie the Pooh walking around, she excitedly ran toward him, yelling over and over, "Pooh, it's me, it's me!" That moment was as real as anything real in the whole wide world to her.

When I was a boy, I had Grill, my toy gorilla. Our son, Matthew, had Griz. The younger boys had special stuffed doggies. The guys still have them, and I have a stuffed gorilla. All of us have to grow up, but I pray that we never *totally* grow up.

In the Bible, I Corinthians 13:11 tells us to put away childlike things when we grow up. Never forget that it doesn't tell you to put away a childlike heart. It's so sad to see how many people grow up and forever put away their childlike hearts. Kids have something figured out that most adults have forgotten: there is power in imagination.

Power of the mind teachers will tell you what Napoleon Hill wrote so eloquently in *Think and Grow Rich*, the 1937 classic. "Whatever the mind can conceive and believe, it can achieve." The Bible tells us to "Call those things that are not, as though they were." (Romans 4:17). When we put all of this into practice, we start living the way we are intended to live. Jesus taught that we must "become as little children" to enter the unseen world (the Kingdom of God).

The magic of a childlike heart and childlike faith is not magic at all. Thoughts, dreams, and creativity are sometimes more real than what is actually real. It's a world of its own. And it's for all of us, as long as we haven't buried our power of imagination. People who can't see past the realities of today are doomed to mediocrity at best. Hopefully, they'll learn this reality: everything that is real now, was at one time only imagined. And what was once imagined was as real as what actually became real. People who created great things in the past, like jet planes, all had big imaginations.

In the beginning, God saw Heaven and earth in his mind, and He spoke them into existence. He then looked to himself as the pattern from which to create mankind. At one time, it all wasn't real. Or was it? The answer is a resounding yes!

Someday, when I pass through Heaven's gates, probably with Grill in my hand, I "see" myself being greeted by departed family members and then seeing Jesus in the distance. I see myself running with wonder and excitement, exclaiming over and over, "Jesus, it's me, it's me." I see it now, therefore I believe it will be so.

What is real? What is not?

It isn't always what has been taught.

What is not? What is real?

It isn't always what you can see, hear, and feel.

HEBREWS 11:1

60

SPEAKING OF GOOD HEALTH

SUNDAY

About three decades ago, during my teaching days, there was a year when I was sick for most of the winter. I still had to work, of course, because it was mostly lingering colds and maybe a light flu. Some of it was because my resistance was down, but I'm convinced now, in hindsight, that much of the problem was that I was talking about it all the time, with anyone who would listen. Statements such as "I can't shake this cold" and "I'm catching everything that comes around this winter" were the focus of my every conversation. I prayed that God would make me well, but I proclaimed to all who would listen that I just couldn't seem to get well. So it didn't work!

You may know people who talk constantly about their bad health. It gets old, doesn't it? Their bad health becomes their identity. It's so counterproductive. Talking about your bad health is like putting fertilizer on weeds.

There are good examples out there as well. We know family and good friends who have battled or are battling some potentially life-threatening health problems. These loved ones are examples of how one *should* behave when faced with such possible devastation. What's the difference between their approach and mine? You almost can't get them to talk about it! One of them lost her battle this summer to cancer. It's a sad fact that sometimes bad things happen to good people who do the right things. But her last months were so honorable. The last few times we saw her, her ground rules were that we wouldn't dwell on her sickness, and we couldn't cry and be sad. We kept our word and had a wonderful, light-hearted visit three days before she passed.

The word "dwell" has two meanings. One refers to where we live. The other refers to thinking or talking about something incessantly. I think they are interrelated. When we dwell on something like sickness, that becomes, in some ways, where we live. And remember, what we focus on, we give power to. So I have an easy-to-remember statement:

"That on which you dwell will swell."

Parents who raise their kids in an overprotective atmosphere, not letting them touch sand and dirt or crawl on the floor, not letting anyone touch them, many times end up with sickly kids. Science has shown that when kids aren't exposed to things that kids like to get into, like sand and floors, they don't develop natural resistance to common germs. We all know that there are extremes in the other direction as well, so keep the floor mopped and make the cat box a no-touch zone.

Don't let bad health become a focus. Talk about good health, think good health, and refuse to let your illnesses become what people will someday remember you for. And never forget, "If you keep worrying about your and your family's health, it will go away."

JAMES 5:14-15

61

YOU ARE MY SUPERHERO

Words have power. We can speak life into others, or we can speak defeat into them. We can also speak into ourselves life and success or death and failure by saying things like, "I'm such a failure, I'm so overweight, I'm such an angry person, I can't do anything right, I'm always sick, my kids can't catch a break…" The list goes on and on. And, if we are not careful, that perceived or real weakness can become our identity. When we speak negative words like that about ourselves or our kids, we are, in some ways, prophesying the future. So it should be no surprise when our life begins to follow those negative words and beliefs.

When we speak into someone else's life, are our words edifying or cutting? I'm reminded of the story of a little boy who had a caring mother who, at bedtime every night, would tell him, "You are my Batman, you are my Superman, you are my Spiderman. You are my Superhero." One night, the family got back late, they had company, and the mom had to send him off to bed without their normal quiet time. A few minutes later, the little boy got out of bed and told his mother, "You didn't tell me who I am." When that little boy starts school, if he doesn't know who he is, he will allow himself to be defined by friends, mean kids, and sadly, even some teachers, coaches, or ignorant adults. So, be cognizant of these questions: What are you saying into others' lives? What are you speaking into your own kids' lives (whether they are still children or adults)? And, maybe most importantly, what are you speaking into your *own* life? Choose Life!

Prov 18:21

62

STRONG FAITH

SUNDAY

E veryone dreams of doing something better. But many never see their dreams become reality. Life can be hard, and it can bury one's dreams deep inside. Eventually, those dreams are buried in the ground with them. Why is that? I believe that many times, it's due to mindset. How you see yourself is vital. The people you associate yourself with will contribute to that mindset as well. I've said it before, and I'll say it again because it is worth repeating: "If you think you can, or think you you can't, you are probably right."

Ponder these five beliefs, as you look to improve your mindset:

1. If you think you are weak, you are right. And with only that belief, you "can't."

2. If you think you are weak but God is strong, you are right. But with only that belief, you still "can't." Lots of people believe that God is strong, but they also believe that God can't use them because of their weaknesses.

3. If you think that you are strong *because* God is with you, you will not only be right, but you "can" accomplish much.

4. If you think you are strong and you associate with people who also believe that, and all of you have God and his strength partnering with you, you "can" make a difference in this world.

5. If you think you are strong and don't need God, the power of positive thinking will work for a season. It may look and feel right, but in the long run it's an illusion. Someday you'll find that you "can't."

So, how do we get strong faith? First of all, we don't need a lot of it (just a mustard seed; Luke 13:18-19), but we should plant that seed and help it grow. How does it grow?

1. Studying the word of God (faith comes by hearing the word of God; Romans 10:17)

2. Hanging out with "can do" people who share your faith and believe in you. There are people who will drive you down and keep you down. Stay away from them. They are poison. They don't want to see you succeed. And remember, there are even a lot of good people who will keep you down.

3. Spend some time each day in prayer, asking God to guide your steps and make them sure as you partner with him with this walk of faith towards your dreams.

4. Be careful of the words you speak. "Death and life are in the power of the tongue." –Prov 18:21. Choose Life!

5. Fill your mind with the "good," such as good books, good movies, and good television shows. Be

informed, of course, but consider cutting down on television and newspaper news. It can drag you down.

In conclusion, we'll return to the word *strong*. People want strong muscles, but few will put in the work to get them. You don't get them without consistent exercise. So it is with our faith muscles. Everyone wants strong faith, but it takes discipline and exercise. Invest a little of your time each day in working your faith muscles, and hang out with people who believe in you and share your strong faith. You'll set the world on fire!

PHIL 4:13:

63

DON'T PUSH, PULL

SATURDAY

Newton's third law says, "For every action there is an equal and opposite reaction." Always remember that when you push people to do what you desire them to do, human nature will cause them to push back. Our family had an older relative who felt it his obligation to tell everyone what they were doing wrong in life. There was nothing wrong with that. In fact, he was a family leader, so it was totally acceptable. The problem was that he felt it was his obligation to tell you that every time he saw you!

As parents of adult children, or as a role model to others, when we see them not quite where they should be, we have an obligation to try to lead them in a better way. But, if we pound them with those words over and over again, Newton's law will kick in, and we will seldom get the results we want. There are four words that start with the letter "P" that we should remember: Pray, Pull, Persuade…but don't Push. You can pull a piece of rope, but you can't push it.

How many people have stubbornly refused to change because people they love pushed them? How many people have turned away from church or even God altogether after being "beat over the head" with the Bible? How many spouses change by being nagged?

So, what is the answer? We can't simply sit back and watch someone we love go over a cliff that is just over the horizon. I believe we need to pray for wisdom to know what to do. We should tell the person and pull them up, using words to persuade them. But, while we love them and are, therefore, obligated to say something, we won't push them. Then, for their own good (and yours), let go and let God. Never give up on them, keep up the prayers, and be there for them if they need you. God usually doesn't push us, but He guides us along this journey of free will. He gives us the perfect template by which to guide others.

～

DEUTERONOMY 31:6

64

ARE YOU TOO POSITIVE?

SUNDAY

I believe that balance is one of the keys to a successful life. Today, I want to focus on getting *out* of balance--toward the good. What do I mean? Well, have you ever known someone who believes in being positive, but after a while, they take it to such an extreme that they are no longer real? That's the person who, no matter what is going on, will always say that life is fantastic, couldn't be better, blah blah blah.

Don't get me wrong, it's great to be positive and speak positively, but a person also has to have credibility. If things aren't going so well for you, just say, "Well, things aren't too good right now, but I believe that it's going to change for the better." That is a real statement with no phoniness, ending on a positive bend.

We once knew a lady once who we thought had the most ideal marriage with the most loving, caring, perfect husband. That's what she would say anyway. After she "dumped" him, we found out the truth. He was a jerk, didn't treat her right, and cheated on her all the time.

Even though she was a nice person, she lost some credibility. Now, I'm not suggesting that she had to put out her dirty laundry for all to see, but she also didn't have to fib and brag about it being opposite what it was in order to make everyone think all was perfect.

I've also known people who so much wanted others to think that they were a person of great faith, that they *never* showed weakness or vulnerability. Again, balance is key. Be positive, but never forget to be real and human. Then, when things are going just great and you tell others as much, you will be believed and trusted. Have a positive bend, but don't bend so much that you eventually break others' trust of you.

JAMES:5:16

SEPTEMBER

"Life's like that sometimes. Now and then, for no good reason a man can figure out, life will just haul off and knock him flat like all of his insides are busted. But it's not all like that. A lot of it's mighty fine, and you can't afford to waste the good part frettin' about the bad. That makes it all bad. You understand what I'm tryin' to get at? When you start lookin' around for somethin' good to take the place of the bad, as a general rule, you can find it."

—Fess Parker, *Old Yeller*

65

DON'T LET YOUR TESTIMONY HURT ANOTHER

SATURDAY

E arlier this year, our son Jeff and his wife Jana, who live in Houston, were looking at homes so they could move out of their apartment. They would find the "perfect" house, get excited, and something would happen such that they couldn't buy it. They were getting discouraged, but I honestly can say that they kept faith and continued to say, "God has the right place for us." Finally, after four or five setbacks, they got into the place they are now living.

When Hurricane Harvey hit, they temporarily moved into their friends' home, which was on a bit higher ground. A week after the hurricane hit, they finally got to go back home. Their home was not flooded or otherwise damaged. The other houses they were looking at *all* flooded, and the apartment complex they were in just a few months prior was underwater. They were so grateful, and they know that their unanswered prayers for other houses were actually answers in their favor.

But that's not what today's Thought is all about. When Jeff and Jana posted on Facebook about all of this, they used such wisdom. They told the story, and acknowledged that many other good people out there didn't fare so well, including friends and fellow church members.

Do you see where I'm going with this?

We have to be very careful that our testimony doesn't become someone else's test. The wonderful things God has done for you can be perceived as a "rejection by God" to another based on what they are going through.

Telling others about how God miraculously spared your child from tragedy can cause a spiritual wound to someone who has tragically lost a child. Bragging about putting your fourth kid through a university can hurt the person who can't afford to send their kid to even a junior college. Telling others how you pray for health, and that God has blessed you with great health, can be hard for someone who has been battling sickness yet praying to get well.

If I show how God has blessed me with a beautiful truck, how would that make others feel? You know, those who have no car and have been hoping, praying, and working for one. Or, those who have prayed for an upgrade for their clunker for months or years. The truth is that God blessed me for sure, but He blessed me because it could be afforded, and to be honest, the credit union was a big part of the blessing!

Facebook is a great tool for keeping up with others and their families. For the most part, people post the good things about their families, myself included. What we don't post much about are the struggles. In past years, we have had family members with drug problems, suicides, rarely straight A's in school, and the need to fight through their own personal battles. But if we aren't careful, it's easy to get the impression that everyone's Facebook families are wonderful and doing great... except for our own. And, once again, we can feel rejected by God.

"But," you may say, "we are supposed to give testimonies." I agree. For what's it's worth, here are some tips. And, at the risk of sounding like a broken record, balance is the key.

- Remember that giving testimonies *is* important. It builds people up and gives them hope.
- Pray for wisdom about sharing a testimony with others. Sometimes only God knows whether what you say will be uplifting or defeating.
- Never let your testimony transform into a boastful attitude. Pride comes before the fall.
- If you are feeling badly because of someone else's testimony, remember that feelings like jealousy and hurt aren't good to hold on to. Try hard to rejoice in others' blessings. Remember , "If He can do it for thee, He can do it for me."

Finally, both good things and bad things happen to

good people, with no particular reason, plan, or pattern. Make the best of every moment. Life is too short for bitterness and envy. Be thankful for what you've got instead of focusing on what's not.

1 Corinthians 13:4

66

WORK NOW, PLAY LATER

SUNDAY

I remember the feeling of a beautiful spring school day when I was in college. I would decide to goof off instead of going to class. I would declare my own holiday; what a blast! I could get some sun and maybe fish or head to Oak Creek. I remember having a feeling of dread when the day was over, knowing that I was going to have to catch up on what I missed, knowing that I put myself in a mess. Life lesson!

Have you ever considered that many negative things we do bring short-term happiness but long-term consequences? Turning that around, many positive things we do are uncomfortable when we do them, but they bring long-lasting positive results. My dad would say, "Work now, play later. Then you can really enjoy playing." That is so true. Overeating feels really good right now. Too much alcohol or drug use can bring short-term good feelings. Skipping a workout or a walk and instead flipping on the TV is really nice! But each of those can have negative results a day later, even disastrous results when it comes to drug use or a consistent habit of only looking at the "now."

Let's turn that around. A person who wants to lose weight can take daily steps in order to lose two or three pounds a month. That may seem trivial—until you see that consistently doing the right things can bring you the loss of twenty-four to thirty-six pounds in one year! Saving money is hard for most, but doing it consistently for many years will set you financially free. When I spend time with God in the morning, read my Bible, feed my mind with a positive book and CD, and make that a priority, it seems like things just start working out for the better, and my day and week both go better. Believe me, it's easier to just flip on the TV or get on the internet than discipline myself to do what I know to be beneficial. It's a battle that I know I must win!

Set some goals, each day, take small steps to get there, and, like my dad said, "Work now, play later." Read the story or watch the cartoon of the Grasshopper and the Ant from *Aesop's Fables* for further reinforcement of this concept.

∽

PROVERBS 6:6-9.

67

BETTER OR BITTER?

SATURDAY

W hen bad things happen in our lives, and you just can't figure out the *why* and the unfairness of it all, you have a choice when it comes to how you react. The question is this: will your choice make you a better person in the long run, or will it make you a bitter person? Are the bad times ones you bring up again and again, almost as though you are building a shrine to them? Or, do you make the choice to *live* again and somehow move on.

I remember my lowest times, especially those times losing family members, and I can honestly say that our family making a choice to live again, to laugh in the midst of the sorrows, to fight to stay positive when everything in us wanted to be negative made all of the difference in getting us through. When we lost our daughter, Dawn, I recall all of the family sitting around the kitchen table the night before the funeral, telling stories and crying, then laughing almost to the point of crying! The laughter was so loud that the neighbors must have thought we had lost it!

In the hour we got the horrible news, I remember Linda giving God thanks, while at the same time, I was mad at God that it happened. I remember Linda honoring her commitment to finish and deliver a wedding cake for a dear friend without even telling the newlyweds of the tragedy—all on the same day we got the news about Dawn.

Fess Parker, the lead actor in the Disney Classic *Old Yeller*, had one of the most powerful lines in the movie. After they had to bury Old Yeller, he said, "Life's like that sometimes. Now and then, for no good reason a man can figure out, life will just haul off and knock him flat like all of his insides are busted. But it's not all like that A lot of it's mighty fine, and you can't afford to waste the good part frettin' about the bad. That makes it all bad. You understand what I'm tryin' to get at? When you start lookin' around for somethin' good to take the place of the bad, as a general rule, you can find it."

It's all about choices. And sometimes, those choices have to precede the feelings. When bad things happen, choose to *live* in the midst of it all. Choose to be better, not bitter. Choose to love, laugh, and even praise God when your insides are telling you to be mad at God and at life. We don't owe a lifetime of grief to anyone or any one situation. We only have one life to live here on this earth. Do you want to be a bitter person, dragging down anyone who will listen? Or do you want your life to be a testimony of being an overcomer, becoming a better person in the long run? Bitter or better, we all have the choice.

∼

Proverbs 3:5-6

68

BIG PICTURE PEOPLE

SUNDAY

A big picture person is someone who looks at things "in the long run" or has a "let's wait and see" approach. They are usually very patient when it comes to big decisions. They are, at times, almost prophetic, as they see things in a futuristic way. Not all people are big picture people, which is good. Having both "big picture" and "now" people make for a good balance, even in the same household.

A big picture person is occasionally misunderstood, even to the point of being criticized. A big picture person usually doesn't get too high during the good times, but they also don't get too low during the tough times. They can be both visionaries and dreamers.

One June day, Linda was looking at our brown back yard lawn. She said we needed to water it. A lot. I wanted to wait, because the monsoons always come in late June or early July. So we compromised and watered a bit. Then, in early July, two weeks of rain totaling nearly five inches magically transformed the grass from brown to green. Which one of us was right? I'd say both.

A big picture person can drive other family members crazy, because they are patient with a certain problem and don't panic. There was a conversation with my dad that took place over and over through the years when he was still with us.

Dad: "What are you going to do about it?"

Me: "I'm not sure yet, but I'm not going to worry."

Dad: "Well you better get to worrying!"

Funny, but true.

Big picture people sometimes believe in giving away some of their money. Some call it tithing. They trust that, in the long run (or big picture) God will take care of them. That philosophy can be criticized by others such as financial advisors or even other family members, who look at the money as necessary in the short term.

Big picture people can be beneficial to have in a household. They're needed to build a family's savings, to get out of debt, and to have a "checks and balances" approach to making decisions. But there is also downside to their presence.

Big picture people can take procrastination to the extreme. They can become so Heavenly, so future-minded, that they aren't of much use in the present. In each of our lives, there are times when something needs to get done *now*. There are seasons when we must give our all, knowing that this kind of opportunity won't pass this way again.

Big picture people can also be the opposite of giving people, becoming a kind of scrooge, not wanting to give or spend money as they try to accumulate for the big picture. The person lives poor, then dies rich, never having used or enjoyed those items he accumulated. Some big picture people don't marry, or never re-marry, as they wait for the perfect person—the one who doesn't ever come along.

If you are a big picture person, ask God to help you to have the wisdom to know when to get 'er done now versus when to have patience. Be open-minded and let others help you stay in balance, but especially ask God for help. Being a big picture person is a blessing. But, as with any gift, it can also become a curse.

If you are a "now" person, ask God to help you to see the value of stepping back and looking at things in the big picture. The making of huge decisions can usually wait until tomorrow or beyond. Don't live your life never learning patience or seldom looking into the future. In this "microwave and tech" age, most people want things now or want to jump into them immediately. They seldom want to wait for the big picture to unfold, which usually doesn't work out well. Jumping from one relationship to another or one marriage to another isn't unusual for the "now" people. They simply do not want to wait.

God works in the now at times. But I have found that God is seldom in a hurry. He knows the big picture of our lives that He wants for us, if we'll only trust and have patience. Keeping that trust during hard times is especially important, as many people turn away from God during those times. They can't see past the hurts of today. I've personally witnessed sad stories of people who didn't trust God during hard times. They turned away and never came back, never knowing what might have been. It's not a wonderful life.

God has a big picture he wants to paint with your life. It will be a beautiful one, but you'll have to see past the muddle of today's hurts as well as today's glow and excitement. You need to let Him guide and direct your steps, and ask Him to help you with your weaknesses while perfecting your strengths. The big picture that will be painted will be your life's story. You will help write the script if you will only have patience, balance, and trust.

GALATIANS 6:9

69

THE THANK YOU NOTE

SATURDAY

Have you ever had friends, or even family, who call you and you are immediately suspicious? You know the type: they only call when they want or need something. Do you ever wonder if God feels the same way about us?

I like the story from many years ago of a frustrated grandma who would send her grandkids cards with money for Christmas, but would never receive a thank you note. The grandpa bet grandma that if he sent them cards *without* money, they would send a thank you note. The bet was on. He sent the cards and in them, he wrote, "Merry Christmas, enjoy the ten dollar bill." Without fail, each one of them wrote a thank you note back saying, "Thank you for the card, but you forgot the ten dollars."

That story illustrates how we all can respond at times, never stopping to thank God for blessings, whether big or small. Then, when the tough seasons of life come, we ask if God has forgotten about us, and it's easy to get mad at God for not caring, even though His love never fails.

I firmly believe that living an attitude of gratitude "pokes holes in the rainclouds of blessings" and living with an ungrateful attitude can keep us "wandering in the wilderness," wondering why God doesn't care. It's all about choices and choosing to be grateful even for the small things, remembering to send God "thank you notes."

1 THESSALONIANS 5:18

70

UNCONDITIONAL GIVING

SUNDAY

Throughout recent hurricanes and forest fire disasters, we have witnessed countless examples of unconditional giving. Neighbors helping neighbors, strangers helping strangers, victims helping other victims—all colors and creeds helping one another, all coming together under the big umbrella called America. It makes me proud.

With Jeff and Jana living in Houston, displaced for a few days, we got an account of the reports of people looking not for a handout but instead looking to lend a hand. Lending a hand is a loose play on words because it is a loan that isn't expected to be paid back. It's an unconditional gift.

In my twenties, I learned a lesson that has stayed with me ever since. I was managing a motel. A young couple came to the desk and asked me for the cheapest room. They said they needed to keep a few dollars back for food and gas. I gave them a ridiculously low price. Later, I felt a nudge in my heart. Even then, I could recognize that the nudge wasn't from me but from God. I had to act. I caught up with the young couple as they were unloading their car and handed them my own money for the amount of the room plus some food money. I knew I had done right.

The next morning, seeing they had left early, I went to get their towels for the laundry. I was shocked upon entering the room. They had stolen all the towels and the blankets. And there were beer cans thrown everywhere, plus an empty bottle of booze on the shelf. That's the thanks I got! And that is where this particular life lesson began for me.

My first reaction was, "I guess I totally misunderstood the nudge last night. I will *never* do something like that again!" Roots of cynicism and bitterness took hold. But then, I heard something in my heart—you know, that feeling when you just know that you are being spoken to with the unspoken words of true wisdom and truth. Here is what I heard: "You did the correct thing. I asked you to give and you did. You can't control how a gift is received. You let me handle them in my own way. When you give, it has to be without any conditions." Cynicism and bitterness were uprooted, and a life lesson was planted in their place.

I believe we are called to be giving people. Something good happens to us deep inside when we give, expecting nothing in return. The Bible tells us to "Give and it shall be given unto you…" In other words, God will take care of you in His own way when you are a giving person. But even that can't be our motive. We should never give to get, even from God. When we give to get, that is trading, not giving. The true heart of giving is unconditional, as is the unconditional love that God gives to us, even when we have made a mess of what we have been given, just like that young couple did.

LUKE 6:38

71

BUCKET LIST ITEM: DONE!

SATURDAY

> "The world stands aside to let any man pass who knows
> where he is going"
> —*Spencer's Mountain*

My high school football coach, Art Sharpe, called me Bart. Not because of my middle name (Barton), but because he knew of my love for the Green Bay Packers, especially legendary quarterback Bart Starr. I have always dreamed of watching a football game at the legendary Lambeau Field, but I was also always told that getting a ticket was an impossible dream; the stadium has been sold out since 1960 with no end in sight! I'll return to this story later.

Many years ago, during a particularly difficult year for us financially, Linda heard of an Iowa group at our son Ron's church that was going to make a two-week trip to the Holy Land a few months later. She had always wanted to go there. The problem was that it would cost a few thousand dollars, and we were having a tough time scraping together a few dollars even to go to a movie. I told her that I thought it was impossible. She said she understood, but she didn't listen! She said she would use only the unexpected money that came to her, and started putting some dollars away.

She started making plans. She put a picture of the Holy Land in the kitchen and looked at it every day. She put the trip on her calendar, and started speaking, acting, praying, and planning as though she were going. She wanted to walk where Jesus walked; I wanted to walk where coach Vince Lombardi walked. You can tell who had their priorities straight!

As a person of "great faith," I supported her fantasy, all the while telling her I thought it was impossible. She may have heard me, but she listened to a higher source. Through yard sales and crazy good spontaneous happenings such as her winning a fancy golf cart in a raffle and selling it, the money was there in the nick of time, and she made her dream trip. I scratched my head in amazement, wondering how the heck that happened, once again showing how much faith I really had (or not!).

But I learned something very important that goes hand-in-hand with one of my favorite quotes. This one is from Johann Wolfgang von Goethe, and it reads, in part: "That the moment one commits oneself, then providence moves too. All sorts of things occur to help one that would never otherwise have occurred. Whatever you can do or dream you can, begin it."

The keys to Linda's dream trip were committing and

beginning. She had none of the *hows* figured out ahead of time. If she would have tried to have all her *t*'s crossed and *i*'s dotted ahead of time, the story of her Holy Land trip would never have been told, because it would never have happened.

As I write this, I'm in Green Bay, Wisconsin. On Sunday, I will be near the 50-yard line in the lower level of Lambeau Field to watch my Green Bay Packers! A year and a half ago, Linda said to start making plans to go. "How?" I asked, once again showing the truth of my "great faith." She just said to plan, and she would support me, just as I supported her Holy Land trip. To keep the story short, here I am in Titletown with my son, Ron! I'll be walking where Vince walked and Bart played. I have this hunch that I'll have Jesus walking right alongside me too, whispering, "Oh ye of little faith. Start listening to your wife!"

James 1:17

72

WHERE WERE YOU WHEN I
NEEDED YOU?

SUNDAY

Does it ever seem like when we seem to need God the most, sometimes we know He is closer than ever, but other times He just doesn't seem to be around? I've said to God out of frustration many times in my life, "Where are you when I need you?"

To illustrate with an analogy, when kids first start playing football early in their school years, coaches are allowed to come onto the field with them during games, showing them where to line up and helping them every step of the way. Later on, as the kids get older, the coaches have to stand on the sideline during games. The team must execute on their own. Similarly, when I taught school, I did my best to prepare the kids, but during the tests, I couldn't help them. Maybe it's that way with God during our times of testing. Remember, faith isn't faith without the testing of that faith. And it's by faith during times of testing that we need to realize that, just like a coach or a teacher, God is there, but He may be quiet in order to see how we execute what He has prepared us for.

Do we pass the test and advance along our walks? Or, do we give up and come up short, needing to retake the test? God's grace will show more patience than any of us can imagine, and during certain tests He will carry us to get us through. But, during many other times of testing, I believe He will watch from the sidelines to see how we perform in the game all on our own.

MATTHEW 25:23

OCTOBER

~

Well there's a dark and a troubled side of life. There's a bright and a sunny side too.

But if you meet with the darkness and strife, the sunny side we also may view.

Keep on the sunny side, always on the sunny side, keep on the sunny side of life.

It will help us every day, it will brighten all the way, if we keep on the sunny side of life.
—*lyrics from an 1800s song written by Ada Blenkhorn*

73

SPEAKING THE TRUTH BUT BELIEVING A LIE

SATURDAY

Y ou can speak the truth and believe a lie with the *same words*. Think about that. Our identity, in our own mind's eye, is who we really are. In Proverbs, the Bible says that as we think we are, we are. So, if a youngster is told his whole life that he is a bad boy (and even goes so far as to wear a shirt that proves it), don't be surprised if that bad boy lives out his identity.

But how do words of truth become a lie? That boy doesn't have to be that bad boy, and in God's eyes, he is something much more valuable than that. When a person says about their weakness, "That's just the way I am," it usually doesn't have to be that way forever, unless it's an incurable condition. One problem I have with Alcoholics Anonymous (a great organization, by the way) is that a person says, "My name is ___, and I am an alcoholic." I wish they would change that phrasing to "recovered alcoholic" or "recovering alcoholic." A weakness should never define our identity, in my opinion.

You may have heard it said, "Don't let your mouth write a check that you can't cash," and I agree—if the words spoken are boastful in nature. But many times, our words write a check that *will be cashed* in the future. "My kids are sickly," "I'm so overweight," "We are always broke," "We'll never get out of debt," "I'm such a loser," "Nobody likes me," and so on. They may all be words of truth to a point, but when we speak them as though they define our identity and believe them to be our true identity, that truth spoken today is a lie when it comes to who we could be. Don't let your words give your mind an excuse to give in and give up. You can be better! I can be better! We are examples that will give our family, friends, and those around us a reason to be better too.

∿

JOHN 1:12

74

KEEP ON THE SUNNY SIDE

SUNDAY

Have you ever gotten up in the morning and shortly afterward, found your mind in turmoil? You have a feeling of dread in your gut. Some call it "getting up on the wrong side of the bed." Or, maybe you woke up in peace, but a few things started happening that weren't perfect, and before you knew it, your peace of mind was gone. Some even post it on Facebook, telling their Facebook world that it's going to be a "crappy day," forgetting that you will claim what you proclaim.

In church last week, the preacher said that where your thoughts go, your heart soon follows. That hit me as truth. Peace of mind is a choice. Happiness is a choice. You have to control your mind, or you will find it controlling you, right down into your heart. And what is in your heart will dictate the way you will live your day, and eventually, your life.

"But," you may say, "you just don't understand my circumstances." Fair enough, but remember that some of the happiest people I've known have had to endure some extremely hard times. And some of the most miserable people I've known have had "silver spoons in their mouths" most of their lives.

When bad things happen, it can be difficult to stay sunny side up. But God calls us to do that, in time. In fact, the Bible tells us that there is a season for mourning. But the Bible *doesn't* tell us that there is a lifetime for mourning. Your hard times or losses can become your identity if you let them. For example, when a loved one passes, that tragedy can double because, in a way, you will die too if you let mourning become your lifestyle. The only difference between the deceased and you is that you are still occupying a body. Remember, you don't owe it to the departed not to get on with your life. In fact, I believe it dishonors their memory to take it past the season of mourning. Would they want that?

So, let's go back to the beginning with all of this. Each day is a gift. Very few of your days will be perfect, and some will be downright crappy. When you feel those weird thoughts rising up to rob you of your peace and joy, especially those thoughts that you get first thing in the morning, try to control them. Because those thoughts, whether good or bad, are seeds that will grow into the tree of your life. That's why some people become bitter, while others just get better and better.

How do we control our thoughts? Each person will find what works best, but what helps me are the following morning steps, which I'm ashamed to say I don't always follow.

- One, seek ye (God) first (Matthew 6:33)
- Two, turn off the news and negative TV shows
- Three, never put on music that isn't uplifting
- Four, try my best to have some quiet time and ask God to bring His peace
- Five, ask God to show me how I can be a divine connection to others this day (helping others takes the focus off of me and my problems)

The 1800s hymn "It is Well With My Soul" was written by Horatio Gates Spafford. He had just lost his four daughters when the ocean liner, Ville du Havre, slipped beneath the Atlantic waters. Days later, he wrote the hymn while searching for the bodies. That sort of peace of mind doesn't come from our strength. It is divine, but we have to ask for the "peace that passes understanding" (Phil. 4:7). Happiness is a choice. Peace is a choice. And the building blocks of peace and happiness are all of your todays, starting today.

Keep on the Sunny Side

Written by Ada Blenkhorn 118 years ago in honor of her disabled nephew, who, with a wonderful attitude, would always say to take him to the "sunny side" when his wheelchair was being pushed. It was later popularized by the famous Carter Family, then was highlighted once again in the 2000 movie, Oh Brother Where Art Though. *Here are the beginning lyrics:*

Well there's a dark and a troubled side of life
There's a bright and a sunny side too
But if you meet with the darkness and strife
The sunny side we also may view
Keep on the sunny side, always on the sunny side
Keep on the sunny side of life
It will help us every day, it will brighten all
       the way
If we keep on the sunny side of life

~

HEBREWS 13:6

75

WHAT I FEARED HAS COME UPON ME

SATURDAY

I n the Book of Job, we learn that Job was a good man in all ways and prospered in all he did. But he lost everything in a series of events. Two things jumped out at me when I read his story. One was that he said that what he had always feared had come upon him. That tells me that he lived much of his life in fear. So, the fear did him no good!

Fear and worry are counterproductive. But what I want to focus on is the reaction of his friends when all these things happened. They immediately came to the conclusion that Job must have done major wrong things in his life or had secret sins. Otherwise, as they reasoned, these things would not have happened to him. Somehow, they thought, God must be punishing him.

And they were dead wrong.

How many people today live their lives with the wrong type of fear of God? They believe that when they do something wrong or don't live their lives properly, God is up there with a scorecard, punishing or rewarding them depending on how good they have been. The problem with that is that it doesn't leave room for God's grace.

Don't get me wrong, there are natural consequences for wrong lifestyles. If you take drugs, they will take you down to the pit. If you are abusive, you'll find yourself alone. If you jump off a cliff wanting to defy the law of gravity, you'll end up dead. These consequences will occur no matter how good of a person you are.

There are also *good* consequences that God has built into the fabric of our natural laws. Give and it will be given to you. Eating right will help you to be healthier. The power of faith works.

So many people really don't have room in their schedules for God or for praying. Then, when bad things happen to them or other people, guess who gets the blame. Yep, God—the one they don't have time to have a relationship with. There are others who have a pretty good relationship with God, but they live their lives against natural laws, thinking that God's grace will take care of them. Like the family who spends money wildly and carelessly then ends up broke and in a mess, all the while wondering why God "didn't care."

In summation, the endpoint is the same flawed philosophy of Job's friends: that God's scorecard rewards or punishes, depending on how good we are. So what do we do? Keep a close relationship in prayer with God, let Him guide your steps and make them sure, then live your life the best you can within the good natural laws that are built into our world. Although things happen to all people, both good and bad, living right within the natural laws and letting God be your guide is a recipe for a good life. The lyric of an old country song I've never liked says, "God's gonna get ya' for that." Don't fall for that nonsense.

1 Corinthians: 15:10

76

THE WISDOM OF FORREST GUMP

SUNDAY

I t's been twenty-three years since the simple wisdom of the movie *Forrest Gump* arrived on the big screen. The power of child-like faith, the love of God's grace and redemption, and the common-sense approach to life made the movie unforgettable to many. Although the movie was fiction, I saw it as one full of core principles of truth.

One line in particular struck me as odd and a little discouraging, but over the years, the more I thought about it, the more I realized that Forrest's wisdom was right on.

"I don't know if we each have a destiny, or if we're all just floatin' around accidental-like on a breeze. But I, I think maybe it's both," Forrest stated.

I, like Forrest Gump, believe that we all have a destiny. That destiny may call you to be a world changer. That destiny may call you to raise or have a good influence on kids, who will pass down value and create an impact for generations to come. Maybe your destiny is simply to make a difference in your own sphere of influence. Or, maybe you are destined to help others achieve *their* destinies. Whether your destiny seems to be small or you are called to reach thousands or millions, you are a vital part of a providential plan to make the world better.

Like Forrest Gump, I also believe that life's breezes can keep us floatin' around, not sure where we are going and not understanding the lessons of where we have been. In other words, we all have a destiny, but we won't see it come to pass if we spend our lives taking the path of least resistance, letting the winds of life take us on jet streams to nowhere, around in circles. I think millions of lives come to an end with these sad questions being asked: "What was my purpose? Why was I here?"

Is it difficult and risky to run against the wind? Absolutely. But we have to come to a point in life when we realize that it's not what we *want* to do that is important, but what we are *meant* to do. When you align yourself with your purpose and destiny, God will partner with you, letting you accomplish much with child-like faith and trust. And, in time, you'll find that what you *want* to do is also what you are *meant* to do. That's living your destiny. Your destiny will become the desire of your heart. And you will discover yourself making a beautiful tapestry of life's "box of chocolates."

ROMANS 12:2

77

DON'T BE SO OPEN MINDED THAT
YOUR BRAINS FALL OUT

SATURDAY

One of my favorite sayings is: "Be open minded, but don't be so open minded that your brains fall out of your head and you lose your common sense." Today, let's look at things with an open mind, while keeping our common sense intact.

Our nation is so polarized. I believe one of the reasons for this is the refusal of both sides to look, with an open mind, at the other side of issues. As a rule, there are good people on both sides. But good people are being divided by people who have a financial or political interest in dividing us. All sides are guilty of using divisive tactics to appease the haters. What happens is that neither side trusts the other, and nobody budges an inch. Closed minds prevail, and nothing gets done. The dividers stay in business. We all lose.

Growing up, a conservative friend of mine was such a great leader. He still is. He went from class president to foreman of a large Hotshot crew to eventually becoming the supervisor of the Tongas National Forest in Alaska, the largest national forest in the nation. But, through his conservatism, Forrest (Cole) taught me something valuable at a class reunion a few years ago. I asked him a question about the Alaskan Pipeline that went through the Denali Wilderness. "There are two sides to this pipeline controversy. Who's right and who's wrong?" His answer was short and to the point, which wasn't surprising since he's always been a guy of few words. He answered simply, "Both."

Now, let's take it from the political realm to the church realm. Sometimes, I just have to shake my head at the mean things that people post on Facebook about certain churches or pastors. The bad things said about a church or pastor by another congregation or pastor is just not the approach Jesus would use, in my opinion. These "religious" people are so judgmental of others. Isn't it interesting that Jesus loved everyone, but the ones he had the biggest issue with were the "religious," judgmental folks of His day? In fact, He once called them a "brood of vipers." Vipers can't be trusted. Vipers will sometimes bite each other. Sound familiar?

Right here in Williams, Arizona, we are doing something that is unheard of in many communities. We get together once a month for a multi-church Sunday evening service. We put our differences aside and come together in unity. It is *very* powerful. Protestants along with Catholics and some Mormons get together under one roof to worship the creator. We put our "religious" attitudes and judgments aside.

Remember, you can't look for the worst in others and expect them to see the best in you. Their political and religious beliefs may not totally line up with yours, but love is the answer, not hate and division. Who's right? Who's wrong? As Forrest would say, "Both."

"Nobody's right if everybody's wrong."
— *"For What It's Worth," 1967 song by Buffalo Springfield*

78

GOOD FEAR, BAD FEAR

SUNDAY

I'm looking forward to our Trick or Treaters because I have a very authentic-looking and scary Velociraptor puppet. Traditionally, I put it on my hand when I pass out candy, and the raptor snaps at their young hands. It's so much fun to see their "flight or fight" reactions. Some jump back (flight), while others slap at it (fight). Linda just shakes her head and rolls her eyes at my weirdness!

These youngsters are simply doing what comes naturally. God has built into all of us an element of fear in order to keep us alive or keep us from getting hurt. It's good fear. Another word for it is caution. While in Houston last week, a near accident prompted a conversation about how close calls or accidents make us better drivers. If you speed all the time and drive recklessly, you can pray all you want, but your approach will eventually catch up to you. Even Jesus spoke about not putting God to the test.

God has also built discernment into us to keep us out

of trouble, to keep us from going broke, or to keep us out of poisonous relationships. That comes as a feeling of caution. When you are feeling that way about a decision you are to make, pay attention! It may keep you from making a terrible business decision. It may keep you from marrying the wrong person. It may keep you from something that only God knows will happen if you go down that road. All of the above are examples of good fear.

Now, let's change directions. There is also bad fear. It's one thing to take precautions in life. That's wisdom. It's quite another thing to live our lives in fear. That's crippling. There is a reason why there are over 365 passages in the Bible telling us to fear not. There is one for every day of the year!

It's been said that fear is the number one enemy of success. Fear wears you down. Fear makes people physically sick. Fear prevents people from getting what they want in life. Fear keeps us from seeing our dreams come true. Fear is a real thing. Too many people say, "It's only in your mind." When that is said, there is a presumption that fear doesn't exist, but it does; it's real. The battles of the mind may well be the biggest battles you will fight in your life.

Finally, and this is the kicker, living our lives in fear is the opposite of living our lives in faith. What happens is, we replace faith with fear, and that becomes our focus. And because what we focus on is what we attract, we bring the bad stuff into our lives!

What's the solution? Ask God for wisdom to know what is good fear as opposed to bad fear. Then ask God to help you to fear not. There are plenty of Biblical examples to choose from. Speak those verses over your life, and make the decision, stubbornly if necessary, to fear not!

II Tim. 1:7

79

PARENTING

SATURDAY

No parent is perfect. We want our children to carry on our good traits, but no parent wants their children to carry on their bad traits. As parents, we want improvement in our children, and then we want more improvement in *their* children, and so on down the line. I believe that is the way it is designed to be. If we make improvements over the way our parents are, or were, that is *not* disrespectful of them. In fact, it's likely the way they would want it.

Here is my point: we all need to quit excusing our negative behavior by saying or thinking, "That's the way my dad was, and that's the way my grandpa was, so that's why I'm the way I am." Your dad and grandpa may have had anger problems, but *you* can be the one to make the change. Do you want your kids and grandkids to carry on with those anger issues? Your mom and grandma may have had unpredictable mood swings. Do you really want to pass that on? Or, do you want to be the one who puts a stop to it? How about addictions?

Generational issues are very real. And, if we try hard to develop the positive traits that have been passed down and make it a point to put the skids on the negative traits, we are both honoring our parents and helping set up our kids and grandkids for success.

My mom was a saint—almost! But you have heard me say that Mom was also a worrier. When it was all said and done, she spent so much of her life worrying about things that seldom ever happened that she made life harder for herself than it needed to be. And, at the risk of getting a bit spiritual, when we worry it is counterproductive because we start putting negative faith to work in our lives. So, to honor my wonderful mother, I have decided that I can't live my life engulfed in worry. I believe she would be proud!

PROVERBS 3:5-6

80

LAURA'S POPCORN BALLS

SUNDAY

I'm reminded of a woman our town lost a few years ago, who lived to be nearly 100 years old. Up until the last months of her life, Laura Cole spent decades doing something special for the kids— both young and old. She made the best popcorn balls and worked on them tirelessly in preparation for the hundreds of trick-or-treaters who made a stop at her home a must.

Laura's labor of love transcended generations, as many of us remembered our own childhoods while bringing our own children, or even grandchildren, to see Laura and experience her very special popcorn balls. She made everyone who came by her house on Sheridan Street feel important and special. And her great attitude was infectious, all year long.

She made a difference in the world in her own unique way. Life is a gift that we all share. The blunt reality is that none of us is going to get out of it alive.

The challenge is to take what we have, large or small, and make a difference, whether we are nine or ninety.

Play the hand you have been dealt, and play it to the fullest. Help others along the way. In your own unique way, make your part of the world a better place, and someday people will remember what you did for them, long after you are gone.

Happy Halloween/Fall Harvest to Laura Cole, who has taken her wonderful attitude to a better place, surely to hear, "Well done good and faithful servant."

MATTHEW 25:23

NOVEMBER

∼

When you truly BELIEVE, your mind goes to work and ideas come to you, guiding your steps and making them sure, taking you along Possibility Road with its twists and turns. But, when you believe something is impossible, your mind goes to work and shows you why you are right, firmly planting a roadblock on Possibility Road.

81

QUE SERA SERA

SATURDAY

I have fond memories of my childhood when my mom would sing the Doris Day song "Que Sera Sera." It was a pretty song, a fun song, and it seemed to deliver some sound philosophical life wisdom. It is often believed that life is predestined, and what will be will be. It's a nice thought, until you think more deeply about it.

There have always been religions and sects that believe that way. In other words, it doesn't matter what you do or don't do, everything is in God's will and control. So why try? You can't change anything anyway.

There are also groups that *don't* believe in the existence of God, and they believe life is fruitless. Therefore, eat, drink, and be merry, for tomorrow you might die. And that's it. There's nothing merry about that!

Some people go through life with the philosophy that everything is controlled by bosses or politicians, so there's no use in trying too hard to change the world.

Take what you can and live for "number one" because "the man" controls everything anyway, and he wants to keep you down.

Here is what I'm asking you this weekend: do you believe in a strict adherence to fate and predestination? If so, why try, why dream, why strive to make the world better? And, here is where I might step on a few toes: why pray for health, protection, and direction, for if it's all going to be God's will and God's decision anyway, why bother? I have always wrestled with that paradox, to some extent. And, although I'm no expert, my conclusion is that we may see a little bit of both during the journey of our lives. But I firmly believe that we can change many circumstances and our world can become a better one by the result of our actions.

Back in the 1970s, it was a common belief and philosophy of many Christian churches that we were living the last days before the return of Jesus. Sound familiar? The reasoning seemed to be Biblically sound given the world events of those days. The common theme was, "We know not the day or time," but it can't go very long. Some even reasoned, in response to a unique Biblical interpretation, that there was no way the world could go past 1988. I was on board with that, and I talked to my mom about it. She told me that in the 1940s, there was a lot of talk that the end of the world was near, World War II was proof, and Hitler "may be the antichrist."

Now, here we are, still alive and kicking as a world. But the point of this writing isn't to prove or disprove the latest end-of-times philosophies. I'm here to say that people who believe that "the end is near" sometimes get into huge debt because they believe that they won't have to pay it back anyway. There is no reason to make long-term plans, goals, or decisions because our time is limited. Therefore, some of them spend and give away lots of money (did you know that tithes go up with end-of-times teachings), take on high-dollar mortgages, and beat everyone over the head with the Bible because "it's almost over, and time is quickly running out." I say that from personal experience. My "end of times" friends in the 1970s spent years recovering from the resulting debts, high mortgages, and losses of credibility.

So, in some ways, Doris Day was right. We have to live our lives according to the song's lyrics: "What will be, will be…the future's not ours to see." But live with the attitude that you can change circumstances, that God has given us free will, and that we have to make the most of our gift of life.

Can we change the will of God? It's an age-old question, but I'm on the side that believes we can, at times (read about Abraham, Moses, Mary, Hezekiah, and others). I feel that God has a purpose for each of us, that God loves us, and He desires for us to live out our purpose and love Him in return, living in His image. That's God's will. But does everyone live their God-given purpose? Does everyone reciprocate God's love? Since the obvious answer is no, we have to also realize that our free will can be used in good ways to make us into exactly what God wants us to be. God wills us to be a certain way, and we don't always follow. But because of His grace, He can help us through all of our mistakes, imperfections, and off-track moments to bring us back around.

Live each day like it's your last. Live each day like Jesus could return at any time. In other words, live like you are leaving or dying, but plan as though you'll be here until you are very old.

Que Sera Sera, but realize that the future *can* be shaped by our todays, so in some ways, the future *is* ours to see because we have a hand in shaping it. And, even though it *might* be so, I refuse to go through my life believing that we're on the eve of the destruction (referring to Barry McGuire's 1965 song, "The Eve of Destruction"). Remember, "the end has been near" for a long, long time.

∽

MATTHEW 24:36

82

PRAYING OUT OF FEAR

SUNDAY

There's lots of fear out there! Today, let's talk about that fear and how to pray the right way.

Now, I'm not saying I'm any kind of expert on prayer, but I have some strong thoughts about the right and wrong ways to pray. One way is to pray out of fear. "God please don't let my child get in a car accident." "Lord, keep me from having a heart attack." I've prayed in somewhat the same format for much of my life, especially when I was younger. But I eventually noticed that when my focus was on the things I was afraid of, eventually those thoughts of fear got lodged into my subconscious and became my focus.

Remember, what we focus on, we attract. I'm not saying that the bad things that have happened to you in your life are your fault or a result of the way you pray. I've said it before: both good and bad things happen; they just do. But I want my faith to be without fear. I want my focus to be on the good, not on my worries.

And I want to pray in such a way that I pray with power.

So, how do I pray now?

I thank God ahead of time for the protection, health, and covenant of blessings for my family. I speak divine health for myself. I know that God's will overrides everything, but when we ask God for our thoughts to become agreeable with His will, many times what we desire is what God desires *for* us. He's just waiting for us to speak it, pray it, and declare it. Never be afraid to ask for the best!

~

JEREMIAH 29:11

83

DOING THE IMPOSSIBLE

SATURDAY

Those who say it's impossible need to get out of the way of those who are on their way to doing it. It is crazy to think about what mankind has accomplished in just over a century —"impossible" things like flying, driving a vehicle, inventing the internet, and hundreds of other impossibilities.

Impossible things do happen, but not with traditional thinking. In fact, traditional thinking blocks the path of the impossible. You have to think outside of the box. Jesus did. He healed people using spit, mud, water, or simply the spoken word. You can't trade faith for a formula because that stifles creativity.

Although there is no formula, there is a pattern relative to those who have accomplished the impossible. The pattern looks like this:

SEE…BELIEVE…SEE.

See: you have to see in your mind's eye what isn't there yet (imagination).

Believe: you have to believe it in your heart (faith).

See: then, you will see it with your own eyes when it happens (accomplishment).

Now, in between these three steps are other important steps. One is to start talking about what you are imagining. Speak as though it's happening. Words activate your faith. Next, start making plans. Then, start taking steps toward your "impossible" dream. You won't yet have all of the "hows" figured out, but you can still take steps, even if those steps are tiny. God will walk with you, but He won't drag you.

You also have to resist people who are resisting you. God won't drag you, but people will, and oftentimes they'll drag you *down*. Many people will resist creative ideas and thinking outside of the box. They'll be more than happy to tell you that it's impossible and that you're crazy. But, if God has set you on a course, don't listen to those negative voices, even if they are only in your head.

In our history, the idea of automobiles was resisted. The idea of flight threw some people into a frenzy, saying that if God intended for man to fly, he would have given him wings. You get the picture.

A few years ago, I formed the first Williams Christmas Committee, and a few of us got together to try to make Williams a Christmas town. One of my goals was to get an ice rink. The trouble was that it would cost a few hundred thousand dollars. We had nothing when we started. But, by putting the above principles to work and sharing the concept with the new Christmas Committee, in a few months we had hundreds of kids and adults skating on Williams' first ice rink. We bought a used rink, ice skates, and a zamboni for a dollar! We were able to ice skate in Williams for a few years.

But it was a little scary at times and looked to be a stupid mistake now and then. For some reason that only God knows, it seems like many times, when you are close to seeing your impossible dream come true, there is a season of discouragement. Maybe it's designed that way to test our seriousness and our faith. Maybe it's resistance from the dark side to make us give up. But this "death of the vision" seems to be a common theme when someone is attempting the impossible. Whatever it is, don't let it rob you of your goal. Remember the old saying, "It's always darkest before the dawn."

When you truly BELIEVE, your mind goes to work and ideas come to you, guiding your steps and making them sure, taking you along Possibility Road with its twists and turns. But, when you believe something is impossible, your mind goes to work and shows you why you are right, firmly planting a roadblock on Possibility Road.

What is *your* impossible dream? Like the song says, you have to "Dream the Impossible Dream." That's the first step (SEE). Maybe your impossible dream is to get out of debt. Maybe your impossible dream is to see your kids excel. Maybe your impossible dream is to write a book. Or, maybe your impossible dream is on a grander scale, one that helps thousands of people.

But a dream is only a dream until you believe it. And believe is only a word until you speak it. And words are only words until you take steps forward. Although those steps won't be easy, perseverance will get you to a time when you finally see it. And, most importantly, a dream come true is only for you until you share it. That will help others take their dreams off of their "shelves of the mind," dust them off, and go for it.

PHILLIPIANS 4:13

84

PUSH EQUALS RESISTANCE

SUNDAY

When I was young, I was taught by older, wiser people, that keeping things in balance was one of the most important lessons of life. When I was in college, there was a particular Christian group that had good intentions. The problem was that the megaphone approach at the activity center day after day made people avoid them like the plague.

I was a Christian, and more than once was I directly told by one of these people that I was going to burn in Hell. They had no balance or people skills. I've seldom seen that philosophy work—in order to bring people to your way of thinking you beat them over the head with your beliefs. That's true whether in religion, politics, Facebook politics, network marketing, or the en vogue issue of the day.

When I was in my twenties and writing for the newspaper, a wise publisher passed some philosophy to his son, who years later passed it on to me. I'll paraphrase: "Politics is like a pendulum. Sometimes it swings left. Sometimes it swings right. Politicians and political parties have a tendency to overreach and take things too far. When that happens, voters are there to help correct it, and get the pendulum swinging the other way."

When you get upset over election results, try to calm down. The voters have spoken. Approaches are going to swing the other way for a while. There are checks and balances built into our system, and if there is an overreach, there are election consequences that will come to pass. All political parties and candidates should remember that balance is key. Push too hard, and you will get resistance.

Whether your political passion is the national election or local races, it is vital to give our leaders a chance to succeed. If you are the praying type, pray for our national, state, and local leaders. We should do that whether we are happy with the results of an election or not. They need wisdom and divine guidance. Those of us who live in this country all want the best for the future. There is power in being united, even in our differences.

EPHESIANS 4:3

85

HANGING OUT WITH TURKEYS

SUNDAY

Choose your relationships wisely. Do they build you up or tear you down? Do they motivate you to do better, or try to keep you where you are? Are they your cheerleaders, or your critics? Do you feel better about who you are by being around them, or do you feel negative about yourself after being around them? Do they encourage you to follow your dreams, or do they make you feel silly for having dreams?

Examine the people you are spending time with. Remember that you are generally only going to be as good as the people you surround yourself with.

Be brave enough to let go of those who are keeping you down. It takes guts to get out of the ruts and even more courage to leave the people who are pulling you in that direction. But it's a choice you should make for your own good.

The Bible says, "For as (a person) thinketh in his heart, so is he." It's hard to soar with eagles when you're hanging with turkeys, unless, of course, you're having Thanksgiving dinner!

PROVERBS 23:7

86

THANKSGIVING: NOT JUST A ONCE-A-YEAR EVENT

SUNDAY

Thanksgiving: it's a lifestyle, not just a once-a-year event. Being thankful through the good and the bad times is a habit that will mold you into a person that people look up to and want to emulate. My son, Jeff, made me a special cord bracelet, a skill he learned in the Army and perfected in the danger zones of Afghanistan. I wear it daily, and when I put it on each day, I use it as a reminder to give thanks. Being thankful makes our lives so much happier.

Anybody can be thankful when all is going well. But many of those same people complain bitterly when bad things happen. Admirable is the person who keeps a right attitude during the hard times, being thankful to God through it all.

I've found that one of the most misunderstood verses in the Bible comes from I Thessalonians 5:18. It says, "In all things give thanks." Other versions say, "Through all things," while a few others say "For all things." My opinion, for what it's worth, is that we should keep a thankful attitude *through* all things, but we don't thank God *for* the bad things that happen.

Bad things do happen. To everyone. When a jetliner crashes, the good and the bad die, of all religions and no religion. But we don't thank God for the plane crash. When we start the impossible lifestyle of thinking we have to thank God for bad circumstances, that's only one step away from blaming God as well. He isn't some grand puppeteer, blessing some, killing others, bringing down planes, and keeping other planes flying.

It's sad to think about how many people don't thank God through the good times but blame him when something bad happens. They say, "If God is so great, why didn't He keep that man from shooting all those people?"

Looking back through the years, I personally don't thank God for the death of my sister, our daughter, or other loved ones. But I don't blame Him either. I will never believe that God came and took them away because, as some say, "He needed another angel in Heaven." Bad things just happen sometimes. What I *can* say is that God helped us through the hard times, and keeping a thankful attitude made the walk easier. I don't understand why these bad things happened, and never will until I'm in Heaven myself, I don't think. But I'm so thankful that we will see our loved ones again because of the horrible death that Jesus experienced. Because of the crucifixion, there was a resurrection, which provided eternal life.

We need to make thanksgiving a lifestyle. When we can do that through the thick and the thin, we will develop our true destiny. King David was only a shepherd boy without Goliath. The lions in the den made Daniel one of the heroes of the Bible. And persecution caused the disciples to flee, bringing the story of Jesus to other lands. If we keep the right attitude through hard times, God can use our test to become our testimony, and our mess will eventually become our message. Through all things keep an attitude of gratitude.

ROMANS 8:28

87

MEMORIES OF THANKSGIVING

SATURDAY

What does Thanksgiving mean to you? Memories from my youth include time with my family, sometimes at home, sometimes at my Grandma Mimmie and Grandpa Paul's, and sometimes at one of my sisters' homes. The parades on TV, the smells of dinner cooking, catching a football game with my dad, four days away from school —all those memories flood my mind. Even before I totally understood the true purpose of the day, I remember a down-deep sense of feeling thankful. I think that is what President Abraham Lincoln foresaw in 1863 when he declared a national holiday to take time to give thanks. An interesting side note regarding Lincoln's proclamation: on Thanksgiving week, exactly one hundred years from the first declared Thanksgiving, our country had to endure the assassination of President Kennedy. We came together as a country and found Thanksgiving during our most difficult of days.

I believe that having a thankful heart through the

good times and the bad times is one of the most important principles of a good life. That attitude of gratitude should be a way of life for us all year long. Sometimes it can be hard to find something to be thankful for, especially when times are tough. But that's when we have to search, pray, and think on it. I can almost guarantee that you will find things to be thankful for. And then, take the time to thank your creator. The Bible says to give thanks through all things. I don't believe that we have to be thankful *for* all things because sometimes there are bad circumstances that happen to all of us. But through those times, God wants us to find things to be thankful for.

When our kids were little, it warmed my heart to see them being thankful for even the smallest of gifts. It made me want to bless them more. When they didn't have a grateful heart, I knew it was time for a life lesson. I believe our relationship with God can be similar. One saying I like is, "Be grateful for the small things, and God can trust us with the tall things."

1 THESSALONIANS 5:18

88

THE WALK OF LIFE

SUNDAY

As you take your journey along life's way,
Where you are today is not where you are to stay.
Walk the good walk, one step after the other,
Taking detours as needed, to help a sister or a
*   brother.*
Just keep moving, even if the way is dark,
For God won't guide a car that is sitting in Park.
Let God guide and direct your steps and make
*   them sure.*
For He is the one that will keep your journey
*   pure.*
God's ways are not always clear, there are times
*   of unbelief and fright.*
But take a step of faith, not fear, toward that
*   small guiding light.*
Keep moving forward, that is a key to life,
For we walk by faith, not by sight."
—Bill Sutton

DECEMBER

∾

Fear gives big shadows to small things. Fear won't take
away tomorrow's troubles, but it will take away today's
peace. In the Bible, the angel said, "Fear not; for behold,
I bring you good tidings of great joy, which shall be for
all people. For unto you is born this day in the city of
David a Savior, which is Christ the Lord."

89

THE GIANT CHRISTMAS BUG

SATURDAY

I'm reminded of a Christmas when our son, Jeff, was a toddler, unable to sleep because of a terrible fear. He screamed in the middle of the night, and I arose from my bed to see what was the matter. He said that he saw a giant bug on the wall of his room. He was pointing to an area directly above the little lighted Christmas tree. I told him that there was no giant bug, and to go back to sleep.

He soon screamed again, and again I had to both tell him and show him that there was no giant bug. The third time he screamed, I was getting mad, and I went into his room to tell him to knock it off. When what to my half-asleep eyes should appear? A foot-long shadow of a bug; as it turned out, Jeff had *much* to fear! A tiny box elder bug was climbing on the Christmas tree, and every time it climbed onto a light, the bug's shadow was projected onto the wall!

Jeff was right, and I felt like the Grinch for getting

mad at him and not believing him. Jeff's story is a lesson for all of us. Fear gives big shadows to small things. Once Jeff saw that it was just a common box elder bug, we had prayer time and he was soon nestled all snug in his bed. He went from fear to faith in minutes. Do you give life to your faith or to your fear? Fear won't take away tomorrow's troubles, but it will take away today's peace.

On the night of Jesus' birth, there were shepherds in the fields, probably looking in wonder at the beautiful star shining through the night. Then an angel appeared, and they were terrified. The angel said, "Fear not; for behold, I bring you good tidings of great joy, which shall be for all people. For unto you is born this day in the city of David a Savior, which is Christ the Lord."

The truth allowed the angel to replace their fear with great joy and faith. Just like the event with Jeff and the box elder bug.

Everyone has fears, so how do we go from fear to peace? First, when those fears start taking over, ask God for help. Let Him show you what is true and what is a lie about your circumstances and your tomorrows. And, perhaps most importantly, quit giving life to your fears by talking about them so much. Doing so gives your fears a much bigger shadow that will follow you wherever you go.

You may have some big fears and big problems, but always remember that you have an even bigger God. Ask Him to help you trade your fears for faith and bring peace to your life, starting this Christmas.

"Glory to God in the highest, and on Earth peace, good will toward men."

~

LUKE 2:14

90

LOOK TO YOUR OPPOSITION TO DISCOVER YOUR DESTINY

SUNDAY

W hen I was growing up, it seemed that nearly all of the movies I loved had a good versus evil element. Peter Pan and Captain Hook. Snow White the Evil Queen. Luke and Darth Vader. Moses and the Pharaoh. There were always bad guys in my beloved Westerns too. Some of the movies were true stories; some were fantasies. But I have found that there is a fine line between fantasy and reality, and they intertwine all the time.

Case in point: I believe that there is a dark side to life. The name I use to represent that dark side is Satan. Others may call it the devil, the inner evil, or something else. So as not to argue the point of what it should be called, let's just use the term "the enemy." I believe that all of us can go down the road to darkness or light here on earth, and many times we can weave in and out of the two. Everyone is capable of both.

Let's return to the movies. Pinocchio was almost turned into a donkey because of his trip to Pleasure

Island. And the hard drinking, foul-mouthed Rooster Cogburn had a big heart buried down deep inside. King David and other heroes of epic Bible stories also had a dark side.

If you believe that there is evil, realize that you have an enemy that tries to keep you from your God-given destiny. If you can't figure out what you are meant to do with your life to make a difference in the world, look closely at how the enemy is battling you. When you get on the right road, opposition will come and there will be some big bumps, potholes, and curves. Many of them are placed there by others, some well-meaning and some who are against you.

You won't be a target until you stand up for something. If you are the person who's always getting kicked in the butt, you are probably out in front. If you have lots of opposition, you may just have lots of potential. The enemy won't fight you so much for where you are as he will for where you're going. He wants to stop you from reaching your God-given dreams.

Do you feel like you have opposition when starting toward your dreams? As you advance to a new and better place in life, do you ever feel like you are under attack? Remember that there are new "devils" at new levels.

Let me challenge you with this: if your life is basically nothing but a smooth ride and you seldom have anything go wrong, you may not be a threat to the enemy. Captain Hook went after Peter Pan because he was a threat. Pharaoh's wrath was toward Moses. The snobby religious people took their anger out on Jesus, because he was about to change the world with a better way of living. There is a big enemy out there, but there is a much, much bigger God who loves you.

I used to say, "I don't get it. I know people who only think of themselves and aren't very good people, and it seems like life is so smooth for them." I now understand why. There is a big picture. And if you walk the walk toward your destiny, you will find that the old Christmas song, "Joy to the World," will have special meaning because your life will bring joy to others as well as to you.

Yes, you have an enemy. And, yes, there will be opposition. But don't focus on the enemy. Instead, focus on the light as you fight the good fight. Never give up, and never give in, because just as in a good Western movie, the good guy will win. And, when it's time, as you ride into the sunset after your race has been run, you'll hear these eternal words, "Well done."

MATTHEW 25:23

91

PAST

SATURDAY

For the next three Thoughts, I'll be citing lessons from a couple of my favorite Christmas movies: *A Christmas Carol* and *It's a Wonderful Life*. We are going to talk about the past, present, and future. I'll address one per lesson. But our focus will always come back to the present.

You see, in your lifetime, the only two days that don't matter much are yesterday and tomorrow. Those two days are important, but only to change our present. Our lives consist of one present day at a time. Each day should be looked at as a gift. For today, however, we'll focus on the past.

In *A Christmas Carol*, Ebenezer Scrooge had to come to a point where he saw the past for what it truly was, and how he had blown it by focusing on money instead of the more important things. He changed his present day because of the conviction from his past. He repented and took a new path.

In *It's a Wonderful Life*, George Bailey became

condemned in his mind because of his past. He basically believed a lie about his life, and he thought his life was worthless and that he himself was worthless. That's condemnation, and that is *not* from God.

Conviction or condemnation? How do you feel about your past? Conviction is meant to bring change for the good, and condemnation is meant to bring about destruction. Conviction made a horrible person, Scrooge, into as good of a man as there ever was. Condemnation took a good man, Bailey, to the brink of suicide. It wasn't until an angel showed him the truth about his past that he made a complete change to an even better man. Once he saw his value, he suddenly had an attitude of gratitude regarding his circumstances and his past instead of feeling like he never made a difference. Once his mind was enlightened, his circumstances hadn't changed, but his attitude about it all did, giving him a new life.

Everyone has baggage. This Christmas, are you going to keep those bags packed, lugging them around and letting them drag you down? Or, are you going to unload your bags, put them away, and be determined to make the most of your Christmas present? The only thing you should carry is a gift, your present day. In other words, your present is your present.

Conviction to change or condemnation to destroy? It's your choice!

∼

ROMANS 8:1

92

PRESENT

SUNDAY

Based on one of his dad's rules for life, legendary basketball coach John Wooden said, "Make today your masterpiece." Another unknown author wrote, "If you lose all your money, you may get it back; but if you lose your time, you never get it back." I've said before that we need to make the best of our circumstances *right now* while we're on our way to where we are going.

For Ebenezer Scrooge in *A Christmas Carol*, and for George Bailey in *It's a Wonderful Life*, their present circumstances didn't change, at least not for the most part. What changed was they themselves. For a while, George Bailey even thought he was on his way to jail, but his newfound joy overshadowed any such possibility.

For today, whether your day is good or bad, you can either make a sacrifice of gratitude and praise, or you can sacrifice your joy, giving in to the troubles of the now.

Never forget, it all starts with your thoughts. You have to think about what you are thinking about. Your thoughts today will eventually build your legacy for this one shot we have at this gift of life. When you take this day and, like Scrooge and George Bailey, go into it with an attitude of gratitude, don't be surprised if you are suddenly used by God to be a help and a blessing to others.

During this Christmas season, if you are only looking inward, you won't see the opportunities to help. Those opportunities are everywhere. And be prepared, because those opportunities will challenge you to do more than you ever thought you could.

On Christmas Eve in *It's a Wonderful Life*, people gave what they had and even gave from their lack in order to give to someone who needed it. Who benefits the most from giving?

The giver, I believe. In fact, scientific studies have shown that when you do good or volunteer to help, there are "feel good" endorphins that are released into your body. And, like a circle, when you give a sacrifice of praise, especially when you don't feel like it, you look outward to help, which causes you to be even more thankful and feel better about your own circumstances. Make sense?

Psalm 39:4 says, "Remind me how brief my time on Earth will be. Remind me that my days are numbered." Why is that written?

To remind us to value today. To remind us to make the most of the Christmas present. When we do that, we will look back at the end of our days and know that it truly was a wonderful life.

~

1 Thessalonians, 5:18

93

FUTURE

SATURDAY

E benezer Scrooge got the opportunity to see his past, and what he saw was terrifying. Just like his deceased business partner, his future included being bound in chains. To make a change, he had to change his todays, and he did.

Many people are anxious to change their future circumstances, but they refuse to change themselves today. Therefore, they remain bound. They aren't bound in actual chains, but the chains of their mind are almost as powerful. Although the story didn't tell us specifically, we all know that George Bailey had a wonderful future. What changed in his todays? Nothing beyond his perception and newfound attitude of gratitude. You can't have a wonderful life and wonderful Christmases yet to come while having a whiny, bad attitude full of complaints.

Like Scrooge and George Bailey, your future Christmases will largely be determined by your todays. Learn from the lessons of the past, decide what type of future you desire, and start making your todays building blocks in the construction of your future.

Take the analogy of putting decorations on a Christmas tree. It won't look good tomorrow without doing the work today. You have to have courage, you have to faith, and you have to put in some effort, because grace alone won't get you there. Discipline yourself, and change your wishbones into backbones. Unlike George Bailey, you won't know if your angel gets wings, but your dreams will, and the bell you hear will be ringing in hope for that great unknown: the Christmases yet to come.

JEREMIAH 29:11

94

WHO IS YOUR CHRISTMAS GUEST?

SUNDAY

Who are you going to invite into your home this Christmas season? If you carry a spirit of offense, you will attract that to you, and the feeling of being offended will find its way into your home. On the other hand, if you carry a spirit of unforgivingness, that feeling will rule your holidays. If you have a spirit of defeat, don't be surprised if a feeling of defeat stops by…and stays. If you have a spirit of rejection, be ready to save a place in your heart; rejection is coming. If you carry a spirit of fear, you are inviting the very thing you fear to stop by.

It's been said that misery loves company, and it's true. All kinds of misery is knocking at your door. The choice is yours when it comes, whether to welcome it in or let it pass by. Everyone gets offended. There are times when everyone battles unforgivingness, feels defeated, and feels rejected. We all have fears at times. But the fact that those bad things are in the neighborhood looking for a home doesn't mean that you have to welcome them in and let them set you up for a destructive holiday season.

If you want to attract love, give it away to others. If you want to attract hope, give someone hope. If you want to let "joy to the world" rule your home, set a special place at the table for joy to dwell. What you give out will come back to you.

The holidays are a bittersweet time for most of us. There are usually both sad and happy feelings as we are visited by the ghosts of Christmas past. Both are there. Both are knocking. Who will you let in? Who will have the honored place at your table?

PHIL 4:8

95

DON'T LET YOUR TESTIMONY BE SOMEONE ELSE'S TEST

SATURDAY

Christmastime is a time for peace and joy. It can also be a time of sadness as the "ghosts" of Christmas pasts hauntingly return to our minds. I know a wonderful local lady who experienced a terrible loss a few years ago. While on her way to a wedding with her five daughters, a traffic collision killed three of the five. She has shared with me that it's especially difficult when well-meaning people talk about God protecting their own child from an accident. The song "Jesus loves me" could include an additional line for those who have experienced loss. Sometimes they hear, "Jesus loves me, but he must love you more."

If God gets the credit for all of the good things, we can easily come close to giving Him all the blame for bad things. A funny statement, "S*** Happens," is right on the money at times. Bad things just happen from time to time. They are not God's fault, not the devil's fault, maybe not anyone's fault. They just happen, to all races and religions. That goes for good things too. Of course, it's sometimes God's intervention and direction that brings us good things. But I'll never believe that God is up there like some playwright, taking out three kids while sparing their mom and two others.

When Brent was a little boy, we received a call that he had collided with a school bus while riding his bicycle home. The back tire of the bus crushed his bicycle, but miraculously, Brent was thrown out of the way, unharmed. You can imagine our relief and gratefulness to God for intervening and saving Brent. A couple of years later, a kind and wonderful young girl from our church, making a flower delivery for her mom, was hit by a train and died. What if, in callous disregard for her mom, I testified to how God had miraculously reached down and saved Brent that day? Can you imagine the hurt feelings that could bring from her toward God? Tell your stories, but be tactful and use wisdom when telling them. You never know what "baggage" the listener may be carrying. The right words can lighten their load, and the wrong words can add to it.

I believe that God did, in fact, intervene to save Brent that day. We always prayed for him, and God answered. But why that sweet girl died while Brent did not, well, those are providential questions that I don't believe we are ever going to have the answers to.

Our own family faced a terrible loss as well. Why did our own daughter die while other daughters in similar situations did not? If you must have answers to these type of questions, you will never have peace, and you can easily begin to believe that God doesn't have your best interests at heart.

Back in the 1980s, I felt an offense toward God for years over the death of my sister. Much of the offense came as a result of words from well-meaning church members.

There is something I like to call spiritual pridefulness. That parent who is always saying that God has blessed her with the perfect kid whom God smiles down on with great favor; you know, the straight-A student who is also the star athlete, and so on, and so on. Listening to her testifying is the mom who has been on her knees praying for years, trying hard to live the lesson, "Bring up a child in the way that they should go." But her child struggles in school, sits the bench in sports, and even gets caught up in drugs and other destructive activities. That second mother can, in her own mind, feel rejected by God.

We all know that sometimes results are rooted in cause and effect. You can't drink a twelve-pack of beer every night and expect long-term good health. But many times, results are simply a reminder that bad things as well as good things just happen for no apparent reason. You can see examples of that in families who raise kids the same way, only to have one turn out great and one go down a wrong road.

People had the audacity to say that God brought down destruction on New Orleans with Hurricane Katrina because He didn't like that city and all of the "bad" things that happen there. This year, we've had storms like Hurricane Harvey hit Texas, Puerto Rico, and other places. If Katrina were God's wrath, then He unleashed His fury on other places as well. People who were praising God in Florida for turning Hurricane Harvey to the west may as well have added, "Houston, you've got a problem."

I'm not advising you not to praise God. I'm not saying that God doesn't sometimes intervene and bring a divine answer. And I'm not suggesting that you don't testify about answers to prayer and God's faithfulness and goodness. But, let your grateful attitude be more of a lifestyle through the good *and* the bad. When giving a testimony, ask for God's wisdom for the right words. Be aware of your audience. Let your testimony be a helping hand to lift people up, not a slap that knocks people down. Don't let your testimony become someone else's test

I Corinthians 13:1-13

96

YOUR WORDS WILL FEED YOUR FAITH OR YOUR FEARS

SUNDAY

A number of years ago, when I was president of the Christmas Committee, we ordered some wrist bands with words written on them. On one side was the word Believe, and on the other was the word Faith. The words were meant to have different meanings to different people. Since hundreds of visitors to Williams would ride the Polar Express, the bands could have meaning from the book and movie. For others, the wrist bands were a reminder to always believe and have faith in the One whose birth we celebrate this time of year.

I wore mine for many years until it finally broke. For me, reading those words helped me put things into proper perspective, not just in December, but every day of the year. It especially reminded me to guard the words that were coming out of my mouth. Would those words build my faith or chip away at it?

I also had to balance what music and television programs I listened to as well as the people in my life I listened to. I had to be careful whom I spent my time with. I talk with my family all the time and try to instill in them this important message: you can't pray positive and speak negative if you want to see your prayers answered.

> *Guard what you listen to,*
> *Put a bridle on the things you say.*
> *Don't let spoken words,*
> *Be in conflict with what you pray.*
> *From your mouth to your ears,*
> *Is a journey of words,*
> *That will feed your faith or your fears.*
> *Your faith will be strong or weak,*
> *Depending on your choice*
> *Of what you decide to speak.*
> *Speak words of hope and truth,*
> *Even if it doesn't feel just right.*
> *Always remember that it's a decision,*
> *To walk in faith, not by sight.*
> —Bill Sutton

Romans 10:17

97

BUCK'S CHRISTMAS CARD

SATURDAY

B elow is a Christmas poem I wrote for the newspaper a few years ago under my pen name, Buckhorn Williams. The pseudonym is after a cowboy character loosely based on my Grandpa Paul Tissaw, who for the most part, lived the life of a Western movie!

Buck's Christmas Card

As I gaze over cattle on a Christmas night,
My eyes are fixed to a star,
The star is giving off a Heavenly light
That comes from the skies afar.
My mind wanders back to a similar scene
Of stockmen way back when,
They called them shepherds, but just like me
They are and always were, stockmen.
The sights they saw and sounds they heard
Some two thousand years ago,

The angels spoke the eternal words,
The star was in the sky so low.
What could give a more peaceful life
To stockmen in the fields at night,
It was the thought of eternal life
That took away death's fright.
They had heard of "The Lamb of God,"
It was a phrase they understood,
A baby in a barn of boards and sod
And a cradle made of straw and wood.
This was Him, the blessed one
The Scriptures had foretold,
And with His birth, it was done,
The angels were proclaiming so bold.
"For unto you a Savior is born,
He is Christ the Lord,"
Angels sang through the hours until morn,
They heard them sing in one accord.
The news gave their spirits a Christmas lift
And made their troubled hearts amend,
For God had given them the first Christmas gift,
Of letting Jesus be their personal friend.
As I sit on my horse and look at the sky
At clouds where the star had shone,
My heart's reassurance tells me why
I will never have to ride alone.
And when my days are over here
And I take that final ride,
I'll holler out a big cheer
'Cause I know He's on my side.
Weep not for loved ones gone

Let not tears make your eyes grow dim,
For if they believe in the power of His love
They are spending Christmas with Him.
Merry Christmas

—Buckhorn Williams (aka Bill Sutton)

98

DON'T MISS YOUR CHRISTMAS
PRESENT

SUNDAY

W hen I was a boy, I counted down the days until Christmas. I couldn't wait! Once Christmas was over, I would look back to those days leading up to Christmas, yearning to go back and live December all over again. But before Christmas, I almost lost the magic of the present by trying to get to the destination. Through the years, I've come to appreciate the Christmas season more than Christmas day. I try to make the most of each day during this special time of year.

One tradition of my childhood was watching *A Charlie Brown Christmas* on television. Even at a young age, I picked up on his quirkiness and lovable life philosophies. He knew the value of living for each day, but his worrisome personality was always on display. Charlie Brown said, "I've developed a new philosophy. I only worry about one day at a time." But he knew that there was a deep meaning to Christmas and that his friends were missing out because they were running around like crazy, letting the busyness bypass what Christmas is all about. It was a cartoon, yes, but the message hit home.

A message not only for the Christmas season but for all year is: don't miss your today trying to get to your tomorrow. And, whatever you do, don't let your worries become a thief that steals your todays. Each day is too valuable to waste away in worry.

Author Corey Ten Boom, who developed her unbelievable story and philosophies in Nazi Germany, said, "Today is the tomorrow you were worried about yesterday." Our today is our gift to us from God, all year long. For December it could be worded, "Our present is our Christmas present." Don't miss your Christmas present.

Charlie Brown had imperfections, as do all of us. But he never lost the true meaning of the season, and he eventually taught others. Linus read from the book of Luke, "For unto you is born this day in the City of David a Savior, which is Christ the Lord." Merry Christmas, Charlie Brown!

Matthew 6:34

99

OUR CHRISTMAS PRESENT IS GOD'S CHRISTMAS PRESENT

SATURDAY

*A December walk in the forest takes my mind for
    a spin,*
*Taking me back through the years of Christmases
    way back when.*
*The smell of a broken needle from a pretty blue
    spruce,*
*Thoughts of a childhood Christmas tree is
    turning my memories loose.*
Now haunted by "ghosts" of Christmases past,
*Of when I was a young boy, oh I wish it could
    last.*
Souls now gone from this life but still real,
*Seared in my mind, sights and sounds that I can
    still see, hear, and feel.*
*Bittersweet are those dreams, how time has
    flown,*
Now, not only me, but my own kids, all grown.
*A startled deer jumping from my stepping on a
    dry leaf,*

Awakens me from my happy daydream, mixed
with a little grief.
Then the realization hits me, like the cold wind's
blast,
That today's Christmas present will be
tomorrow's Christmas past.
I want to build memories from today,
Help me to value the present, I pray.
"The Christmases yet to come,"
Will quickly be upon us, here, and then gone.
The clock to Christmas is ticking away,
The years, they're fleeting, I wish they could stay.
But like a toy soldier, time marches by,
If this life is all there is, then there is no reason
to try or ask why.
But a joy awakens deep within my heart,
Telling me that loved ones here and gone will
never part.
Today, yes today, is the day that the Lord has
made,
He IS that baby in the manger, now I don't have
to be afraid.
Christmas in Heaven, or Christmas right here,
Christmas with Jesus is genuine Christmas cheer.
Now walking step by step in the packed white
snow,
No longer walking by myself, but with my savior
I go.
Don't yearn for the past or worry about
tomorrow,

*God's Christmas present to us is THE present
  that brings with it no sorrow.
Merry Christmas to all, and to those in
  Heavenly places,
The true Joy to the World brings smiles to all
  our faces.*

--Bill Sutton, Christmas 2016

100

DO YOU "GET IT?"

SUNDAY

I n *The Polar Express*, the conductor says, "Seeing is believing. But sometimes, the most real things in the world are the things we can't see."

The Conductor "gets it."

At the end of the movie *Peter Pan*, George Darling, the kids' dad, sees the pirate ship cloud in the sky. He says, "You know, I have the strangest feeling I've seen that ship before...a long time ago, when I was very young."

He no longer "gets it," but for a moment it came back to him.

We have a saying in our house that we "get it." And we pray we never lose it. Linda calls me her Peter Pan husband, who never grows up. There is a childlike faith and wonder of the unseen world, and even the childhood fantasy world.

I believe that the unseen world and much of fantasy is as real as anything tangible. But not everyone "gets it."

Maybe they once did, just like George Darling. But over the years, life has happened, and people have told them to "get real." What was once a soft and open heart is now calloused on the outside and hard to penetrate.

When you talk to someone in the last days of their life, many will talk about the fantasies of their childhood, defeating all of the villains while riding the range. Those images are so real that they are seared in their minds forever, and in many cases, they have shaped their adulthoods. So, don't tell me that the unseen world isn't real. It is as real as anything in this "real" world, where fake is the norm.

The creative minds of those who "get it" bring our world gifts of fantasy through movies and books that touch the heart. When the teenage boy in *Toy Story 3* leaves home with his friends, he takes one last look at his childhood toys, and his heart is torn. Will he ever "get it" again?

In *Babes in Toyland*, a line in the theme song says of Toyland, "Once you pass its borders, you can ne'er return again." That thought has brought a lump to the throat of more than one adult as they see their kids leave that magical place. The parents wonder with sadness if they will ever "get it" again.

God's kingdom is the kingdom of the unseen. When speaking of children, Jesus said, "The kingdom of God belongs to such as these." Childlike faith touches the heart of God. When we touch the heart of God, our creativity opens up, our faith increases, and faith becomes a "substance of things hoped for, the evidence of things not seen." (Hebrews 11:1). The unseen becomes real. Do you "get it"?

Throughout my life, especially when I was younger, I've been told to "get real" by many well-meaning people. But I've chosen to follow examples from others who have never gotten real and who "get it": Charles Dickens (*A Christmas Carol*), Chris Van Allsburg (*Polar Express*), Disney, Spielberg, Lincoln, Mother Theresa, the list is long.

One common trait is that each knew that unseen visions could never be achieved by "getting real," and that a creative heart could only be tapped by one who "gets it" and has chosen to do what others couldn't. The above examples have fantasy woven with reality because I think that the line between the two is very thin.

The narrator of *Polar Express* says, "At one time most of my friends could hear the bell, but as years passed it fell silent for all of them. Even Sarah found one Christmas that she could no longer hear its sweet sound. Though I've grown old, the bell still rings for me, as it does for all who truly believe."

Yes, Santa, there are still some of us "Virginias" who "get it" and still hear the bell. And although I can't return to Toyland, there is a place I try to go daily. The entry requirement is simply childlike faith.

"......there is a veil covering the unseen world which not the strongest man, nor even the united strength of all the strongest men that ever lived, could tear apart. Only faith, fancy, poetry, love, romance, can push aside that curtain and view and picture the supernal beauty and glory."

--excerpt from the 1897 New York newspaper article titled, "Yes, Virginia, There is a Santa Claus."

∽

MATTHEW 18:3

ACKNOWLEDGMENTS

This book is dedicated to all of you who have encouraged me to combine my weekly Thought for the Weekend posts into a book. Dozens of you have suggested that I do so, but a few of you have kindly prodded a bit more, which is exactly what I needed to get this book off the ground. I wouldn't have done it without you! Lynn, Deb, Fred, Suzy, Gerry, Sheryl, Janice, Dorene, Yae, Carol, Monica, Emmett, Peggy, Aspen, Jimmie, and a few others have stayed on me the longest and the loudest, and you haven't let go of your vision for me. Also, those of you in my immediate family have been a constant encouragement. Thank you! For son Brent, who helped with the cover design concept, I love your talents and vision.

My wife Linda has been my main cheerleader in every way. Not only that, she surprised me with an anniversary gift, using her own money to get this book off the ground.

Cathy H. Smithers, my cousin and the author of two

books (with another on the way as of this writing), gave me some concrete tips for successfully writing a book.

My editor and publisher, Elizabeth Lyons, "gets it" and understands my *why* when it comes to the reasons to write and publish my first book. The author of five books herself and a mother of five children, she has the life experiences to guide me in the right direction with valuable advice. She was recommended to me by Eddie Aguilar, who has just published his first book, *Lasting Impact: Navigating the Rippling Effects of Suicide*.

My kids and grandkids are my legacy, so this book is an altar I can pass down to them, hoping and praying that they will be able to gain some wisdom as they navigate the journey of life.

Most of all, I want to thank God for the ideas for my Thoughts. For each of them, I prayed that the ideas would come and that the words would be provided. I asked specifically for words that would touch the hearts of the readers. It's my prayer that this book does the same.

ABOUT THE AUTHOR

Bill Sutton was born and raised in Arizona, eventually graduating from Northern Arizona University in 1977. He taught school for nine years. After teaching, Sutton was a Justice of the Peace and Magistrate in Arizona for twenty years, retiring in January 2011. While being on the bench in Williams, he was the presiding Justice of the Peace in Coconino County for twelve years.

Judge Sutton was selected as the MacEachern Award recipient, given annually by the National Judges Association as the "Outstanding Non-Attorney Judge in the United States." A year later, in 2005, Judge Sutton received the "Outstanding Contribution to the Arizona Courts Award," given annually to one or two individuals in the Arizona Court System by the Chief Justice of the Supreme Court of Arizona. He has also been president of the Arizona Justice of the Peace Association and the National Judges Association.

Presently, Judge Sutton is retired from the bench, and he is the founder and president of Wise Choice Alternatives, a court sentencing alternatives company. He is also Arizona Director of American Community Corrections Institute (ACCI), which provides life skills for defendants in the form of self-directed study.

Sutton also founded and has served as the president

of Yes I Can, Inc., which provides motivational and success seminars for youth in the areas of positive cognitive change and suicide prevention.

Ten years ago, Sutton founded and was the first President of the Williams Christmas Committee, At the time of this writing, he has been Chair or Co-Chair of the Committee for four of those years.

Bill Sutton wrote weekly columns and articles for the *Williams News* for a number of years in the early 1980s. He now writes a weekly Facebook blog called Thought for the Weekend, a concept that serves as the foundation for this book.

facebook.com/bill.sutton2

COMING SOON...

Thoughts for the Weekend, Volume 2 is planned for a 2021 release.

Made in the USA
Middletown, DE
10 January 2022